Learning to Read
Using the
BOOK OF MORMON

VOLUME 1
1 NEPHI TO 2 NEPHI 26

Learning to Read
Using the
BOOK OF MORMON

VOLUME 1
1 NEPHI TO 2 NEPHI 26

Creative Application
by Camille Funk

ISBN 13: 978-1-59955-002-2

Published by Horizon Publishers, an imprint of Cedar Fort, Inc., 2373 W. 700 S., Springville, UT, 84663
Distributed by Cedar Fort, Inc., www.cedarfort.com

Cover design by Nicole Williams
Cover design © 2007 by Lyle Mortimer

Printed in China

10 9 8 7 6 5 4 3 2 1

Printed on acid-free paper

Dedication

First, I dedicate this book to my family whom I love very much and who have done their best to support and raise me in the gospel. I also wish to dedicate this book to two very influential people in my life, Ray Bence and Tom Valletta. Ray Bence, who always believed in me and helped me to see myself at a young age the way the Lord sees me. Tom Valletta, my stalwart mission president, who fostered my love for the scriptures and has been my unfailing cheerleader.

Table of Contents

Preface

Using the Book of Mormon to Learn to Read is a two-step approach outlined in three volumes. Step one (which includes the first and second volumes—1 Nephi through Helaman) addresses the phonological approach to learning. Step two (which includes the third volume—3 Nephi to Moroni) addresses vocabulary development.

PART 1—Phonics
(1 Nephi–Helaman)

Research shows that children are most susceptible to learning between the ages of two to six. Volumes 1 and 2 will take that early zest for learning and funnel it into the scriptures and couple it with the tools needed to learn how to read. Each chapter of the Book of Mormon has been carefully outlined to reinforce the development of phonological skills as well as the development of sight (memorization) words, thus combining both the whole language and phonological approach in reading education.

Volumes 1 and 2 will take you carefully through word patterns used in the very early grades and progress up to phonological rules, parts of speech, and sentence structure. Every lesson plan is meant to be repetitive—for the convenience of both the child and the parent. Research shows that children love to adapt to repetition and structure, and common sense shows that all mothers have their hands full. Thus, repetition is also for the ease of the parent.

These volumes have been carefully thought out. Each lesson is structured into a ten- to fifteen-minute learning period every day (for each child). Each main category in every lesson plan (at the beginning of each chapter) is outlined in this section in detail. The following is meant to be used as a reference:

SIGHT (MEMORIZATION) WORDS: These are the words highlighted in green. Sight words are words that must be memorized because they do not follow any obvious phonological rule. Some schools and reading specialists refer to them as power words, sight words, or the whole language approach. As you progress to new chapters you will see more and more green words. Each chapter will build on what has already been learned. These words are printed on practice cards (included at the beginning of the manual) so as to review them on a continual basis, like so:

yea

(Note: Some words follow a rule that is explained much later in the manual, which will be noted. But due to the frequency of its usage, it is initially introduced as a sight word. Once the rule is learned in later chapters, the word will switch from green to blue. Also, as new phonics rules are learned that apply to green words, in most cases the new word form of the sight word will also be in green.)

PATTERN WORDS: These are the words highlighted in blue. As you progress to new chapters, you will see more and more blue words. Each chapter will build on what has already been learned. In each lesson plan, you will either see the first or second option depending upon the chapter.

OPTION 1: 1 Nephi–Words of Mormon: You will see a table introducing a pattern:

Pattern	-on
Patterns in scriptures	**on**
Location in chapter	Verse 26
Exceptions to the rule	gone
Other words made from this pattern not found in chapter	Don, Ron

Pattern: Patterns are the development and extension of the phonological rules that will be learned in each chapter. Each chapter will have a phonological rule that is learned in association with the word pattern. The pattern word systematically takes the phonological rule and breaks it down into bite-sized pieces.

Patterns: Words found in the chapter that are made from the word pattern. (Some chapters will not have an example.)

Location in the chapter: The verse that the pattern word is located in.

Exceptions to the rule: Words that do not follow the word pattern or rule and are most likely sight (memorization) words.

Other words made from this pattern not found in chapter: These are words made by the word pattern that are not found in the chapter, many of which are found in later chapters of the Book of Mormon.

OPTION 2: Mosiah–Helaman: You will see a table introducing a pattern (Table 1) or a rule (Table 2):

Table 1

Pattern or rule	-ay or schwa
Patterns in scriptures	**say, may, way or** awaits
Larger words containing the rule, but not highlighted in chapter	(none)
Location in chapter	Verses 3–6, 9–10
Other words made from this pattern not found in chapter	day, play, today, nay

Table 2

Pattern or rule	Syllable stress—abstract vowels
Patterns in scriptures	**rejoice, power**
Location in chapter	Verses 9, 14–15
Other words made from this pattern not found in chapter	anew, poison, bounty, council, counsel, devour, doubtful, fountain, mountain, profound, tower, author, because, daughter, haughty, awful

Pattern or rule: There are two variations of what could be seen in this box.

    1) Pattern (schwa will be highlighted in orange): (same as option 1)

    2) Rule: Rules do not often come in clean-cut, small words that progress developmentally. The examples of the rules in each chapter will be underlined. Many times the words underlined will be difficult, and some will be hard for the children to read—but the rules are specifically placed so that as we progress through each chapter we can build on the phonological rules taught. Thus, each rule will be underlined in red, only within that chapter, to teach and emphasize the rule.

Patterns: (same as option 1)

Larger words containing the rule but not highlighted in chapter: Words that are too big for a child to read on his or her own but still have the pattern or rule.

Location in the chapter: (same as option 1)

Exceptions to the rule: (same as option 1)

Other words made from this pattern not found in chapter: (same as option 1)

PRACTICE WORKSHEET: There will be a variety of worksheet activities seen throughout volumes 1 and 2.

The most common activity (mostly seen in volume 1) is a word pattern development activity. Using the word pattern letters (given in the beginning section of the manual), place letters or blends in the blank space. On the blank spaces provided, the student can write all the combinations that make a word. (For example: bad, Dad, fad, had, lad, mad, pad, rad, sad, Tad, glad, Chad.) When students find words that are nonsense words (or words that do not exist in the English language), you can help them determine if these are real words by asking them to define the words or put them in a sentence. Nonsense words should not be totally discouraged because they are part of the development in sounding words out.

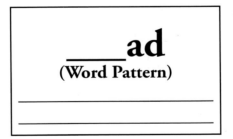

PHONICS RULES: Most chapters will have a specific phonics rule and definition that the reading is trying to reinforce. It is important to establish a firm base with letter sounds and vowel sounds (both short and long).

READING CHUNKS (red lines): Each chapter in the Book of Mormon has a different length. Young children are not prone to being able to sit for long periods of time. Thus, each chapter is broken down into reading chunks—separated by red lines—to break up reading into age appropriate reading portions. Each child is different, and you will have to gauge your child to tell if he or she can or will read more or less.

Each section has a box to check off once it is completed and a place to date it. This is to help the child feel a sense of accomplishment. There is also a space for notes—this is for the parent to make notes about what their child might struggle with so as to reinforce it later. This is related to the educational idea of the "running record." This running record is important because it is a journal entry tracking the progress and needs of your child. This can be used as a firm database in working with school teachers as well.

GOSPEL PRINCIPLE REVIEW/ACTIVITY: Each chapter has a short activity or question that helps the child internalize what he or she is reading. This reinforces comprehension. Do not be discouraged if your child does not show great signs of comprehension early on—most likely he or she is working hard to get words right, but as he or she begins to read more words, the activities will be developed to deepen the child's comprehension and adaptation of the gospel principles taught in the chapter.

PART 2—Word Study
(3 Nephi–Moroni)

It is important to make the transition, once the phonological development is in place, to a deeper study of words. There is no doubt that a parent will teach the meaning of words as they read with their child up to this point. However, this portion will focus on word study or a vocabulary study of specific words chosen in each chapter to help deepen meaning and knowledge of words used in the Book of Mormon. Each section will have the following:

WORD STUDY (VOCABULARY WORDS): Words are carefully selected to enhance the meaning in each chapter and to the doctrines of the gospel. It is suggested to have these words on flip cards for easy review. As the student progresses, the red words highlighted will be added upon. Each vocabulary word will be on a vocabulary word card for easy study and review.

GOSPEL PRINCIPLE REVIEW/ACTIVITY: This continues the idea that the scriptures are more than just a good story but are meant to be applied and studied. There will be review questions (without answers) that are meant to help with comprehension. Some questions will require a more in-depth study using other books of scripture. The activities are geared toward making fun, personal applications that will help the child understand gospel doctrine and principles.

JOURNAL: There will be a section for the student to write their feelings, comments, and questions while they read the chapter. This piece is to promote interaction with the text and a deeper understanding to truly "liken the scriptures unto themselves."

Readers with Learning Disabilities

It should be stated in the beginning that **each child struggles to learn in different ways**. Sometimes you can classify these different learning styles into groups. One of the most common things I have noticed as an elementary teacher is that often times children are either 1) misdiagnosed or 2) not diagnosed.

This section is not intended to become a self-analysis for stereotyping. But it is intended to assist those parents and guardians who find that there might be a significant learning pattern in a child that could use further attention. The wonderful thing about this manual is that you will have a firsthand (documented in the columns) account of how your child reads. From there it is suggested, if particular behaviors are discovered that hinder a child's progress, that you take the information you have collected and consult a licensed professional to help make the correct diagnosis.

If you find that your child does indeed need additional help with learning to read, this section seeks to offer suggestions in dealing with these learning difficulties. First, let's start with discovering signs of learning disabilities (again, please note that not all of these result in an exact diagnoses):

Symptoms

LD Online (www.ldonline.org) is a learning disabilities online resource. The following description is given of key signs of learning disabilities during each life phase[2]:

Preschool

- Speaks later than most children
- Pronunciation problems
- Slow vocabulary growth, often unable to find the right word
- Difficulty rhyming words
- Trouble learning numbers, alphabet, days of the week, colors, shapes
- Extremely restless and easily distracted
- Trouble interacting with peers
- Difficulty following directions or routines
- Fine motor skills slow to develop

Grades K–4

- Slow to learn the connection between letters and sounds
- Confuses basic words (*run, eat, want*)
- Makes consistent reading and spelling errors including letter reversals (*b/d*), inversions (*m/w*), transpositions (*felt/left*), and substitutions (*house/home*)
- Transposes number sequences and confuses arithmetic signs (+, −, x, /, =)
- Slow to remember facts
- Slow to learn new skills, relies heavily on memorization
- Impulsive, has difficulty planning
- Unstable pencil grip
- Trouble learning about time
- Poor coordination, unaware of physical surroundings, prone to accidents

Grades 5–8

- Reverses letter sequences (*soiled/solid, left/felt*)
- Slow to learn prefixes, suffixes, root words, and other spelling strategies

- Avoids reading aloud
- Trouble with word problems
- Difficulty with handwriting
- Awkward, fist-like, or tight pencil grip
- Avoids writing assignments
- Slow or poor recall of facts
- Difficulty making friends
- Trouble understanding body language and facial expressions

High School Students and Adults

- Continues to spell incorrectly, frequently spells the same word differently in a single piece of writing
- Avoids reading and writing tasks
- Trouble summarizing
- Trouble with open-ended questions on tests
- Weak memory skills
- Difficulty adjusting to new settings
- Works slowly
- Poor grasp of abstract concepts
- Either pays too little attention to details or focuses on them too much
- Misreads information

Symptoms Specific to Dyslexia and ADD

Dyslexia: Early Indicators of Reading Difficulty[1]

- Poor phonemic awareness
- Difficulty segmenting words
- Difficulty with rhyming
- Poor letter-name recall/word retrieval
- Difficulty learning and discriminating between sounds
- Ability to read short stories from memory, but inability to read the same word in isolation.
- Early speech and/or language difficulties
- Poor spelling

ADD: Early Indicators of Reading Difficulty[2]

- Inattention
- Hyperactivity
- Impulsivity
- Restlessness
- Distractibility

Learning Suggestions

There are two main learning disabilities found in schools today: dyslexia and ADD. It is recommended that you consult with a physician to find a path that will allow for the most effectual results for your child.

The following are some suggestions for readers that struggle with these learning disabilities:

Dyslexia: Dyslexic students have to use all their senses to be able to cement a word into their minds. Educators call it the multi-sensory approach.

1) **Sight words** (or words without any logical phonological reasoning) are the hardest for dyslexic students and simply need to be memorized. (Practice with the flip cards each day; they need to keep seeing that word to cement it into their mind.) You will find this to be the hardest part of learning to read, but frequent repetition will be the key to memorization.

2) **Word patterns** have a three-step approach.

    a. Tap—This is an important step for dyslexic students to do when learning to read. This is done by taking the thumb and touching the thumb with each finger as the student says the sounds of the word. For example: c-a-t (tap the thumb to the index finger for the "c" sound, the middle finger for the "a" sound, and the ring finger for the "t" sound). This step should be repeated until the child can perform a "swoop" under the fingers used to tap. The swoop is a continual, fluid motion that allows the child to read without cadence, making the effectual sound of the word.

    b. Word building—This is done by making alphabet cards (as found in the preface section for the word patterns) and using these cards to build the word. As the children say the sound, they will place the correct letter on the table.

    c. Say-Tap-Write—This final step will cement the pattern into the child's memory, since he or she not only hears and touches but also writes it. One last time, the child will tap the word, then say the word, and then write the word. Children with dyslexia work well with order. If this process is followed, it will organize information as they input new words.

ADD (Attention Deficit Disorder): ADD students struggle to maintain attention. In order to accommodate this learning need, volumes 1 and 2 have tried to break up the reading sections into small reading chunks.

    1) **Small Reading Chunks:** You will need to gauge your students to determine if they need to be broken into even smaller sections.

    2) **Repetition:** If you notice that your student is not grasping a concept, instead of dwelling on the negative, simply review each day (even if you continue to move forward with other phonics lessons). If you use repetition, the concept has a high likelihood of setting in their minds, and if approached with this simple review technique (lasting about one minute each day), they will also have a lower resistance to allowing the concept to be grasped. Volume 1 (1 Nephi to Mosiah) is set up for thorough repetition, so as to establish a firm phonics base.

    3) **Short Time Frame:** Frustration or lack of interest comes when a task becomes draining and mundane. The idea is to keep the daily reading to five- to ten-minute periods over a consistent daily routine. That way, if students know each day that they only have to read for five to ten minutes, it will less likely become a drudgery.

    4) **Success Chart:** When you focus on what students have accomplished by logging their progress with a success chart, they will have an extra boost of positive reinforcement to help them combat the potential frustration.

Reading Schedule

Reading Assignment	Day	Personal Check-off	Reading Assignment	Day	Personal Check-off
1 Nephi 1:1–3	1		1 Nephi 7:8–12	37	
1 Nephi 1:4–7	2		1 Nephi 7:13–15	38	
1 Nephi 1:8–12	3		1 Nephi 7:16–19	39	
1 Nephi 1:13–14	4		1 Nephi 7:20–22	40	
1 Nephi 1:15–17	5		1 Nephi 8:1–4	41	
1 Nephi 1:18–20	6		1 Nephi 8:5–9	42	
1 Nephi 2:1–4	7		1 Nephi 8:10–13	43	
1 Nephi 2:5–8	8		1 Nephi 8:14–18	44	
1 Nephi 2:9–11	9		1 Nephi 8:19–23	45	
1 Nephi 2:12–15	10		1 Nephi 8:24–33	46	
1 Nephi 2:16–19	11		1 Nephi 8:34–38	47	
1 Nephi 2:20–24	12		1 Nephi 9:1–3	48	
1 Nephi 3:1–4	13		1 Nephi 9:4–6	49	
1 Nephi 3:5–8	14		1 Nephi 10:1–3	50	
1 Nephi 3:9–11	15		1 Nephi 10:4–7	51	
1 Nephi 3:12–15	16		1 Nephi 10:8–10	52	
1 Nephi 3:16–19	17		1 Nephi 10:11–13	53	
1 Nephi 3:20–24	18		1 Nephi 10:14–16	54	
1 Nephi 4:1–3	19		1 Nephi 10:17–18	55	
1 Nephi 4:4–7	20		1 Nephi 10:19–22	56	
1 Nephi 4:8–11	21		1 Nephi 11:1–5	57	
1 Nephi 4:12–15	22		1 Nephi 11:6–8	58	
1 Nephi 4:16–20	23		1 Nephi 11:9–13	59	
1 Nephi 4:21–26	24		1 Nephi 11:14–19	60	
1 Nephi 4:27–30	25		1 Nephi 11:20–24	61	
1 Nephi 4:31–34	26		1 Nephi 11:25–28	62	
1 Nephi 4:35–38	27		1 Nephi 11:29–31	63	
1 Nephi 5:1–4	28		1 Nephi 11:32–34	64	
1 Nephi 5:5–8	29		1 Nephi 11:35–36	65	
1 Nephi 5:9–12	30		1 Nephi 12:1–3	66	
1 Nephi 5:13–16	31		1 Nephi 12:4–7	67	
1 Nephi 5:17–22	32		1 Nephi 12:8–11	68	
1 Nephi 6:1–3	33		1 Nephi 12:12–16	69	
1 Nephi 6:4–6	34		1 Nephi 12:17–19	70	
1 Nephi 7:1–3	35		1 Nephi 12:20–23	71	
1 Nephi 7:4–7	36		1 Nephi 13:1–5	72	

Reading Schedule

Reading Assignment	Day	Personal Check–off	Reading Assignment	Day	Personal Check–off
1 Nephi 13:6–10	73		1 Nephi 17:1–3	109	
1 Nephi 13:11–14	74		1 Nephi 17:4–7	110	
1 Nephi 13:15–19	75		1 Nephi 17:8–10	111	
1 Nephi 13:20–23	76		1 Nephi 17:11–14	112	
1 Nephi 13:24–26	77		1 Nephi 17:15–18	113	
1 Nephi 13:27–29	78		1 Nephi 17:19–20	114	
1 Nephi 13:30–32	79		1 Nephi 17:21–23	115	
1 Nephi 13:33–35	80		1 Nephi 17:24–28	116	
1 Nephi 13:36–39	81		1 Nephi 17:29–31	117	
1 Nephi 13:40–42	82		1 Nephi 17:32–35	118	
1 Nephi 14:1–3	83		1 Nephi 17:36–40	119	
1 Nephi 14:4–7	84		1 Nephi 17:41–43	120	
1 Nephi 14:8–11	85		1 Nephi 17:44–46	121	
1 Nephi 14:12–14	86		1 Nephi 17:47–49	122	
1 Nephi 14:15–17	87		1 Nephi 17:50–52	123	
1 Nephi 14:18–22	88		1 Nephi 17:53–55	124	
1 Nephi 14:23–26	89		1 Nephi 18:1–4	125	
1 Nephi 14:27–30	90		1 Nephi 18:5–8	126	
1 Nephi 15:1–5	91		1 Nephi 18:9–12	127	
1 Nephi 15:6–11	92		1 Nephi 18:13–15	128	
1 Nephi 15:12–14	93		1 Nephi 18:16–19	129	
1 Nephi 15:15–18	94		1 Nephi 18:20–23	130	
1 Nephi 15:19–23	95		1 Nephi 18:24–25	131	
1 Nephi 15:24–28	96		1 Nephi 19:1–3	132	
1 Nephi 15:29–32	97		1 Nephi 19:4–6	133	
1 Nephi 15:33–36	98		1 Nephi 19:7–10	134	
1 Nephi 16:1–4	99		1 Nephi 19:11–14	135	
1 Nephi 16:5–9	100		1 Nephi 19:15–20	136	
1 Nephi 16:10–13	101		1 Nephi 19:21–24	137	
1 Nephi 16:14–17	102		1 Nephi 20:1–5	138	
1 Nephi 16:8–21	103		1 Nephi 20:6–10	139	
1 Nephi 16:22–25	104		1 Nephi 20:11–16	140	
1 Nephi 16:26–29	105		1 Nephi 20:17–22	141	
1 Nephi 16:30–34	106		1 Nephi 21:1–5	142	
1 Nephi 16:35–37	107		1 Nephi 21:6–10	143	
1 Nephi 16:38–39	108		1 Nephi 21:11–16	144	

Reading Schedule

Reading Assignment	Day	Personal Check-off	Reading Assignment	Day	Personal Check-off
1 Nephi 21:17–21	145		2 Nephi 6:11–13	181	
1 Nephi 21:22–26	146		2 Nephi 6:14–18	182	
1 Nephi 22:1–5	147		2 Nephi 7:1–5	183	
1 Nephi 22:6–10	148		2 Nephi 7:6–11	184	
1 Nephi 22:11–16	149		2 Nephi 8:1–7	185	
1 Nephi 22:17–21	150		2 Nephi 8:8–14	186	
1 Nephi 22:22–26	151		2 Nephi 8:15–19	187	
2 Nephi 1:1–5	152		2 Nephi 8:20–25	188	
2 Nephi 1:6–9	153		2 Nephi 9:1–5	189	
2 Nephi 1:10–13	154		2 Nephi 9:6–9	190	
2 Nephi 1:14–20	155		2 Nephi 9:10–14	191	
2 Nephi 1:21–25	156		2 Nephi 9:15–18	192	
2 Nephi 1:26–32	157		2 Nephi 9:19–25	193	
2 Nephi 2:1–5	158		2 Nephi 9:26–29	194	
2 Nephi 2:6–10	159		2 Nephi 9:30–39	195	
2 Nephi 2:11–14	160		2 Nephi 9:40–43	196	
2 Nephi 2:15–20	161		2 Nephi 9:44–48	197	
2 Nephi 2:21–25	162		2 Nephi 9:49–54	198	
2 Nephi 2:26–30	163		2 Nephi 10:1–6	199	
2 Nephi 3:1–5	164		2 Nephi 10:7–13	200	
2 Nephi 3:6–11	165		2 Nephi 10:14–19	201	
2 Nephi 3:12–16	166		2 Nephi 10:20–25	202	
2 Nephi 3:17–21	167		2 Nephi 11:1–8	203	
2 Nephi 3:22–25	168		2 Nephi 12:1–7	204	
2 Nephi 4:1–6	169		2 Nephi 12:8–14	205	
2 Nephi 4:7–12	170		2 Nephi 12;15–22	206	
2 Nephi 4:13–20	171		2 Nephi 13:1–8	207	
2 Nephi 4:21–28	172		2 Nephi 13:9–15	208	
2 Nephi 4:29–35	173		2 Nephi 13:16–28	209	
2 Nephi 5:1–7	174		2 Nephi 14:1–6	210	
2 Nephi 5:8–14	175		2 Nephi 15:1–7	211	
2 Nephi 5:15–20	176		2 Nephi 15:8–14	212	
2 Nephi 5:21–28	177		2 Nephi 15:15–23	213	
2 Nephi 5:29–34	178		2 Nephi 15:24–30	214	
2 Nephi 6:1–5	179		2 Nephi 16:1–7	215	
2 Nephi 6:6–10	180		2 Nephi 16:8–13	216	

Reading Schedule

Reading Assignment	Day	Personal Check-off	Reading Assignment	Day	Personal Check-off
2 Nephi 17:1–7	217		2 Nephi 26:25–30	253	
2 Nephi 17:8–16	218		2 Nephi 26:31–33	254	
2 Nephi 17:17–25	219		2 Nephi 27:1–5	255	
2 Nephi 18:1–8	220		2 Nephi 27:6–10	256	
2 Nephi 18:9–16	221		2 Nephi 27:11–15	257	
2 Nephi 18:9–16	222		2 Nephi 27:16–22	258	
2 Nephi 18:17–22	223		2 Nephi 27:23–27	259	
2 Nephi 19:1–7	224		2 Nephi 27:28–35	260	
2 Nephi 19:8–16	225		2 Nephi 28:1–6	261	
2 Nephi 19:17–21	226		2 Nephi 28:7–12	262	
2 Nephi 20:1–8	227		2 Nephi 28:13–18	263	
2 Nephi 20:9–14	228		2 Nephi 28:19–25	264	
2 Nephi 20:15–23	229		2 Nephi 28:26–32	265	
2 Nephi 20:24–34	230		2 Nephi 29:1–4	266	
2 Nephi 21:1–8	231		2 Nephi 29:5–8	267	
2 Nephi 21:9–16	232		2 Nephi 29:9–14	268	
2 Nephi 22:1–6	233		2 Nephi 30:1–5	269	
2 Nephi 23:1–10	234		2 Nephi 30:6–11	270	
2 Nephi 23:11–17	235		2 Nephi 30:12–18	271	
2 Nephi 23:18–22	236		2 Nephi 31:1–6	272	
2 Nephi 24:1–7	237		2 Nephi 31:7–12	273	
2 Nephi 24:8–15	238		2 Nephi 31:13–16	274	
2 Nephi 24:16–23	239		2 Nephi 31:17–21	275	
2 Nephi 24:24–32	240		2 Nephi 32:1–5	276	
2 Nephi 25:1–4	241		2 Nephi 32:6–9	277	
2 Nephi 25:5–8	242		2 Nephi 33:1–5	278	
2 Nephi 25:9–13	243		2 Nephi 33:6–10	279	
2 Nephi 25:14–17	244		2 Nephi 33:11–15	280	
2 Nephi 25:18–20	245		Jacob 1:1–5	281	
2 Nephi 25:21–26	246		Jacob 1:6–10	282	
2 Nephi 25:27–30	247		Jacob 1:11–19	283	
2 Nephi 26:1–1–5	248		Jacob 2:1–6	284	
2 Nephi 26:6–9	249		Jacob 2:7–10	285	
2 Nephi 26:10–14	250		Jacob 2:11–15	286	
2 Nephi 26:15–18	251		Jacob 2:16–22	287	
2 Nephi 26:19–24	252		Jacob 2:23–29	288	

Reading Schedule

Reading Assignment	Day	Personal Check-off	Reading Assignment	Day	Personal Check-off
Jacob 2:30–35	289		Jarom 1:5–9	325	
Jacob 3:1–5	290		Jarom 1:10–15	326	
Jacob 3:6–9	291		Omni 1:1–5	327	
Jacob 3:10–14	292		Omni 1:6–10	328	
Jacob 4:1–4	293		Omni 1:11–14	329	
Jacob 4:5–8	294		Omni 1:15–19	330	
Jacob 4:9–13	295		Omni 1:20–25	331	
Jacob 4:14–18	296		Omni 1:26–30	332	
Jacob 5:1–6	297		Words of Mormon 1:1–4	333	
Jacob 5:7–11	298		Words of Mormon 1:5–9	334	
Jacob 5:12–17	299		Words of Mormon 1:10–13	335	
Jacob 5:18–21	300		Words of Mormon 1:14–18	336	
Jacob 5:22–26	301		Mosiah 1:1–4	337	
Jacob 5:27–31	302		Mosiah 1:5–8	338	
Jacob 5:32–37	303		Mosiah 1:9–13	339	
Jacob 5:38–43	304		Mosiah 1:14–18	340	
Jacob 5:44–47	305		Mosiah 2:1–5	341	
Jacob 5:48–53	306		Mosiah 2:6–9	342	
Jacob 5:54–59	307		Mosiah 2:10–14	343	
Jacob 5:60–64	308		Mosiah 2:15–20	344	
Jacob 5:65–70	309		Mosiah 2:21–26	345	
Jacob 5:71–74	310		Mosiah 2:27–30	346	
Jacob 5:75–77	311		Mosiah 2:31–35	347	
Jacob 6:1–6	312		Mosiah 2:36–40	348	
Jacob 6:7–13	313		Mosiah 3:1–6	349	
Jacob 7:1–5	314		Mosiah 3:7–11	350	
Jacob 7:6–11	315		Mosiah 3:12–17	351	
Jacob 7:12–17	316		Mosiah 3:18–21	352	
Jacob 7:18–23	317		Mosiah 3:22–27	353	
Jacob 7:24–27	318		Mosiah 4:1–4	354	
Enos 1:1–6	319		Mosiah 4:5–8	355	
Enos 1:7–12	320		Mosiah 4:9–13	356	
Enos 1:13–17	321		Mosiah 4:14–18	357	
Enos 1:18–22	322		Mosiah 4:19–23	358	
Enos 1:23–27	323		Mosiah 4:24–27	359	
Jarom 1:1–4	324		Mosiah 4:28–30	360	

Reading Schedule

Reading Assignment	Day	Personal Check-off	Reading Assignment	Day	Personal Check-off
Mosiah 5:1–5	361		Mosiah 13:26–31	399	
Mosiah 5:6–9	362		Mosiah 13:32–35	400	
Mosiah 5:10–15	363		Mosiah 14:1–6	401	
Mosiah 6:1–7	364		Mosiah 14:7–12	402	
Mosiah 7:1–7	365		Mosiah 15:1–7	403	
Mosiah 7:8–12	366		Mosiah 15:8–12	404	
Mosiah 7:13–16	367		Mosiah 15:13–19	405	
Mosiah 7:17–20	638		Mosiah 15:20–25	406	
Mosiah 7:21–25	369		Mosiah 15:26–31	407	
Mosiah 7:26–33	370		Mosiah 16:1–6	408	
Mosiah 8:1–6	371		Mosiah 16:7–15	409	
Mosiah 8:7–11	372		Mosiah 17:1–7	410	
Mosiah 8:12–16	373		Mosiah 17:8–13	411	
Mosiah 8:17–21	374		Mosiah 17:14–20	412	
Mosiah 9:1–4	375		Mosiah 18:1–6	413	
Mosiah 9:5–10	376		Mosiah 18:7–11	414	
Mosiah 9:11–14	377		Mosiah 18:12–16	415	
Mosiah 9:15–19	378		Mosiah 18:17–22	416	
Mosiah 10:1–5	379		Mosiah 18:23–28	417	
Mosiah 10:6–10	380		Mosiah 18:29–35	418	
Mosiah 10:11–15	381		Mosiah 19:1–8	419	
Mosiah 10:16–22	382		Mosiah 19:9–14	420	
Mosiah 11:1–5	383		Mosiah 19:15–21	421	
Mosiah 11:6–11	384		Mosiah 19:22–29	422	
Mosiah 11:12–16	385		Mosiah 20:1–6	423	
Mosiah 11:17–22	388		Mosiah 20:7–12	424	
Mosiah 11:23–29	389		Mosiah 20:13–18	425	
Mosiah 12:1–4	390		Mosiah 20:19–26	426	
Mosiah 12:5–10	391		Mosiah 21:1–7	427	
Mosiah 12:11–16	392		Mosiah 21:8–14	428	
Mosiah 12:17–24	393		Mosiah 21:15–20	429	
Mosiah 12:25–29	394		Mosiah 21:21–25	430	
Mosiah 12:30–37	395		Mosiah 21:26–30	431	
Mosiah 13:1–6	396		Mosiah 21:31–36	432	
Mosiah 13:7–14	397		Mosiah 22:1–5	433	
Mosiah 13:15–25	398		Mosiah 22:6–11	434	

Reading Schedule

Reading Assignment	Day	Personal Check-off
Mosiah 22:12–16	434	
Mosiah 23:1–8	435	
Mosiah 23:9–15	436	
Mosiah 23:16–24	437	
Mosiah 23:25–31	438	
Mosiah 23:32–39	439	
Mosiah 24:1–6	440	
Mosiah 24:7–11	441	
Mosiah 24:12–18	442	
Mosiah 24:19–25	443	
Mosiah 25:1–8	444	
Mosiah 25:9–13	445	
Mosiah 25:14–18	446	
Mosiah 25:19–24	447	
Mosiah 26:1–7	448	
Mosiah 26:8–13	449	
Mosiah 26:14–22	450	
Mosiah 26:23–29	451	
Mosiah 26:30–39	452	
Mosiah 27:1–5	453	
Mosiah 27:6–10	453	
Mosiah 27:11–15	454	
Mosiah 27:16–21	455	
Mosiah 27:22–27	456	
Mosiah 27:28–31	457	
Mosiah 27:32–37	458	
Mosiah 28:1–4	459	
Mosiah 28:5–11	460	
Mosiah 28:12–16	461	
Mosiah 28:17–20	462	
Mosiah 29:1–7	463	
Mosiah 29:8–13	464	
Mosiah 29:14–20	465	

Pronunciation Guide

Symbol Key

a, e, i, o, u *(lower case)*—Short vowels

A, E, I, O, U *(upper case)*—Long vowels

R *(uppercase)*—Consonant names

ə *(Schwa)*—Translates to "uh" sound, see Alma 20

/ou/—Abnormal sound *(house)*

/ow/—Abnormal sound *(now)*

/oi/—Abnormal sound *(join)*

/oy/—Abnormal sound *(joy)*

/ŏŏ/—Abnormal sound *(good)*

Note: all consonant blends will be noted by slashes (example: /sh/)

Similar Letters and Sounds

Symbol	Example
Short A	
a	apple
Short E	
e	bed
Short I	
i	pin
Short O	
o	hot
al	talk
au	haul
aw	saw
Short U	
u	rug
Long A	
A	cake
ai	paid
ay	way
ei	their
ey	they
Long E	
E	these
ee	feed
ea	speak

Symbol	Example
Long I	
I	kite
ie	pie
igh	high
y	by
ye	bye
Long O	
O	hope
oa	oath
ow	grow
Long U	
ue	True
ui	ruin
ew	drew
oo	food
Abnormal sounds	
/ŏŏ/	good
/ou/	house
/ow/	now
/oi/	join
/oy/	toy

Note: see the Pronunciation Guide in the Book of Mormon for names of people and places.

Sight words

Sight Word	Pronunciation		
I	I	gold	gOld
a	A & ə	me	mE
o	O	our	/ou/r
the	thə	evil	Evil
go	gO	son	sən
do	dU	walk	wok
yea	yA	thee	thE
of	əv	out	/ou/t
as	az	over	Ovr
ye	yE	said	sed
or	Or	no	nO
my	mI	so	sO
is	iz	what	wut
he	hE	few	fU
his	hiz	death	deth
to	tU	among	ə-məng
from	frəm	down	d/ow/n
wo	wO	know	nO
you	U	any	enE
want	wont	most	mOst
be	bE	some	səm
by	bI	how	h/ow/
are	R	give	giv
all	ol	many	men-E
her	hr	your	yOr
we	wE	sign	sIn
were	wr	done	dən
one	wən	other	ə-thr
who	hU	come	cəm
kind	kInd	very	ver-E
have	hav	move	mUv
put	pr	Jesus	jE-sus
buy	bY	live	liv
says	sez	good	g/ŏŏ/d
also	olsO	there	ther
		else	els

Sight Word	Pronunciation
wild	wI-ld
she	shE
even	Ev-en
Zion	zI-un
behold (beheld)	bE-hOld bE-held
has	haz
father	fother
been	ben
both	bOth
half	haf

swear	swer
fro	frO
love	luv
was	wƏz
body	bodE
heart	hrt
began (begin, begun)	bEgan bEgin bEgun
word (work)	wrd wrk

Pattern Letters

a	b	c	d	e
f	g	h	i	j
k	l	m	n	o
p	q	r	s	t
u	v	w	x	y

Pattern Letters

z	bl	cl	fl	gl
pl	sl	br	cr	pr
tr	sc	sk	sm	sn
sp	st	sw	tw	ch
sh	th	wh		

Sight (Memorization) Word Cards

I	a
O	the
go	do
yea	of
as	ye

Sight (Memorization) Word Cards

or	my
is	he
his	to
from	wo
you	want

Sight (Memorization) Word Cards

be	by
are	all
her	we
were	one
who	kind

Sight (Memorization) Word Cards

have	**put**
buy	**says**
also	**gold**
me	**our**
evil	**son**

Sight (Memorization) Word Cards

walk	thee
out	over
said	no
so	what
few	death

Sight (Memorization) Word Cards

among	**down**
know	**any**
most	**some**
how	**give**
self	**your**

Sight (Memorization) Word Cards

sign	done
other	come
very	move
Jesus	live
good	there

Sight (Memorization) Word Cards

else	wild
she	even
Zion	behold
has	father
been	both

Sight (Memorization) Word Cards

half	**swear**
fro	**love**
was	**body**
heart	**began**
word	**work**

Phonics Rule Cards

Short vowel sounds

The sound of the letter phonetically (versus the long sound or name of the letter).

- The short sound of A (example: apple)
- The short sound of E (example: bed)
- The short sound of I (example: hit)
- The short sound of O (example: hop)
- The short sound of U (example: cup)

Consonant-Vowel-Consonant

Taking letters, phonetically saying them out loud, and bringing the sounds together to form words.

Blend-Vowel-Consonant

A blend is the combination of two (or more) consonants together. The blends are BL, CL, FL, GL, PL, SL, BR, CR, DR, FR, GR, PR, TR, SC, SK, SM, SN, SP, ST, SW, TW.

Consonant Diagraph

Two letters that make one sound.

- *"TH" sound*—makes two sounds, for example: 1) the, 2) forth
- *"CH" sound*—for example: **ch**ip
- *"SH" sound*—for example: **sh**ip
- *"WH" sound*—for example: **wh**ip

Complex Consonants

Blends that include three consonants, two consonants that sounds like a single letter, and consonant and vowel clusters. (The complex consonants are QU, TCH, CK.)

Doublet

A special type of across-syllable pattern in which the two consonants are the same.

- LL—for example: ba**ll**

The Silent E Rule—Long Vowel Sounds

When an E is at the end of a word, the E is silent and it makes the vowel to the left say its name (or the long vowel).

[When other rules apply to the word, a word that ends in E is still silent. For example: serve (see R-controlled vowels).]

Examples:
- The long sound of A (example: **a**te)
- The long sound of E (example: h**e**re)
- The long sound of I (example: k**i**te)
- The long sound of O (example: p**o**ke)
- The long sound of U (example: **u**se)

Double Vowel-Long Vowel Sounds

When two vowels are together, the first vowel says its name and the second vowel is silent. (When two vowels go walking, the first one does the talking.)
- The long sound of E (example: **ea**ch)
- The long sound of I (example: p**ie**)
- The long sound of O (example: b**oa**t)
- The long sound of U (example: s**ui**t)

R-Controlled Vowel Patterns

Vowels that are followed by an R are influenced by the R sound.

- The R-controlled vowel sound of A (example: c**ar**)
- The R-controlled vowel sound of E (example: h**er**)
- The R-controlled vowel sound of I (example: b**ir**d)
- The R-controlled vowel sound of O (example: s**or**t)
- The R-controlled vowel sound of U (example: b**ur**n)

Complex Consonants

Blends that include three consonants, two consonants that sound like a single letter, and consonant and vowel clusters. (The Complex Consonants are QU, TCH, CK, GN, MB, KN, WR).

Silent Consonant:

- GN—the G is silent (example: **gn**at)
- MB—the B is silent (example: co**mb**)
- KN—the K is silent (example: **kn**ot)
- WR—the W is silent (example: **wr**ap)

Sound alike final consonant sounds:

- GE and DGE—these blends make the same sound (example: a**ge** and e**dge**)
- K, CK, and KE—these blends make the same sound (example: lin**k**, ba**ck**, ba**ke**)

Soft Consonants:

- *G*—when G is followed by E, I, and Y it makes the J sound /j/ (example: **ge**m, **gi**st, **gy**m)
- *C*—when C is followed by E, I , and Y it makes the S sound /s/ (example: ri**ce**, **ci**ty, **cy**st)

Rules

- *C*—comes before A, E, and U (can, cop, cup)
- *K*—comes before I and E (kit, key)

Complex Long Vowel Sounds

Long vowels make the sounds of their names, but these complex long vowels do not contain the letter of the sound they are making. For example, "vein" makes the long A sound, but the vowels that combine to make the long A sound are "ei."

- Long A (ei, ey)
- Long I (y/ye, igh)
- Long O (ow)
- Long U (oo)

1 Nephi

Chapter 1

Sight (Memorization) Words

I	a	O

Word Pattern

Pattern	-ad
Pattern words in scriptures	**had**
Location in chapter	Verses 1, 7, 14–15, 18, 20
Other words made from this pattern not found in chapter	bad, Dad, fad, lad, mad, pad, rad, sad, glad, grad

Phonics Application

- *Short vowel sounds:* the sound of the letter phonetically (versus the long sound or name of the letter).
  - The short sound of A (example: **a**pple)
- *Consonant-Vowel-Consonant:* taking letters, phonetically saying them out loud, and bringing the sounds together to form words.

Recommended (Age Appropriate) Reading Chunks

- Verses 1–3
- Verses 4–7
- Verses 8–12
- Verses 13–14
- Verses 15–17
- Verses 18–20

Gospel Principle Review/Activity

- Who are Nephi's parents?
- What language is the plates originally written in?
- What did Nephi's father see in a vision?
- *Activity:* Nephi wrote the story of his family. We do the same in a journal. With your parents, start your own journal.

Word Patterns

_ad

Lesson 1: words made with –ad word pattern.
Use alphabet letters to create words.

1 Nephi 1

1 I, Nephi, having been born of goodly parents, therefore I was taught somewhat in all the learning of my father; and having seen many afflictions in the course of my days, nevertheless, having been highly favored of the Lord in all my days; yea, having had a great knowledge of the goodness and the mysteries of God, therefore I make a record of my proceedings in my days.

2 Yea, I make a record in the language of my father, which consists of the learning of the Jews and the language of the Egyptians.

3 And I know that the record which I make is true; and I make it with mine own hand; and I make it according to my knowledge.

4 For it came to pass in the commencement of the first year of the reign of Zedekiah, king of Judah, (my father, Lehi, having dwelt at Jerusalem in all his days); and in that same year there came many prophets, prophesying unto the people that they must repent, or the great city Jerusalem must be destroyed.

5 Wherefore it came to pass that my father, Lehi, as he went forth prayed unto the Lord, yea, even with all his heart, in behalf of his people.

6 And it came to pass as he prayed unto the Lord, there came a pillar of fire and dwelt upon a rock before him; and he saw and heard much; and because of the things which he saw and heard he did quake and tremble exceedingly.

7 And it came to pass that he returned to his own house at Jerusalem; and he cast himself upon his bed, being overcome with the Spirit and the things which he had seen.

8 And being thus overcome with the Spirit, he was carried away in a vision, even that he saw the heavens open, and he thought he saw God sitting upon his throne, surrounded with numberless concourses of angels in the attitude of singing and praising their God.

9 And it came to pass that he saw One descending out of the midst of heaven, and he beheld that his luster was above that of the sun at noonday.

10 And he also saw twelve others following him, and their brightness did exceed that of the stars in the firmament.

11 And they came down and went forth upon the face of the earth; and the first came and stood before my father, and gave unto him a book, and bade him that he should read.

12 And it came to pass that as he read, he was filled with the Spirit of the Lord.

Notes

Date _____
☐ Completed

Date _____
☐ Completed

Date _____
☐ Completed

13 And he read, saying: Wo, wo, unto Jerusalem, for I have seen thine abominations! Yea, and many things did my father read concerning Jerusalem—that it should be destroyed, and the inhabitants thereof; many should perish by the sword, and many should be carried away captive into Babylon.

14 And it came to pass that when my father had read and seen many great and marvelous things, he did exclaim many things unto the Lord; such as: Great and marvelous are thy works, O Lord God Almighty! Thy throne is high in the heavens, and thy power, and goodness, and mercy are over all the inhabitants of the earth; and, because thou art merciful, thou wilt not suffer those who come unto thee that they shall perish!

15 And after this manner was the language of my father in the praising of his God; for his soul did rejoice, and his whole heart was filled, because of the things which he had seen, yea, which the Lord had shown unto him.

16 And now I, Nephi, do not make a full account of the things which my father hath written, for he hath written many things which he saw in visions and in dreams; and he also hath written many things which he prophesied and spake unto his children, of which I shall not make a full account.

17 But I shall make an account of my proceedings in my days. Behold, I make an abridgment of the record of my father, upon plates which I have made with mine own hands; wherefore, after I have abridged the record of my father then will I make an account of mine own life.

18 Therefore, I would that ye should know, that after the Lord had shown so many marvelous things unto my father, Lehi, yea, concerning the destruction of Jerusalem, behold he went forth among the people, and began to prophesy and to declare unto them concerning the things which he had both seen and heard.

19 And it came to pass that the Jews did mock him because of the things which he testified of them; for he truly testified of their wickedness and their abominations; and he testified that the things which he saw and heard, and also the things which he read in the book, manifested plainly of the coming of a Messiah, and also the redemption of the world.

20 And when the Jews heard these things they were angry with him; yea, even as with the prophets of old, whom they had cast out, and stoned, and slain; and they also sought his life, that they might take it away. But behold, I, Nephi, will show unto you that the tender mercies of the Lord are over all those whom he hath chosen, because of their faith, to make them mighty even unto the power of deliverance.

Notes

Date _____
☐ Completed

Date _____
☐ Completed

Date _____
☐ Completed

1 Nephi

Chapter 2

Sight (Memorization) Words

the	oh

Word Pattern

Pattern	-am
Pattern words in scriptures	**Sam**
Location in chapter	Verses 5, 17
Other words made from this pattern not found in chapter	dam, ham, jam, Pam, ram, yam, scam, spam, swam

Phonics Application

* *Short vowel sounds:* the sound of the letter phonetically (versus the long sound or name of the letter).
  * The short sound of A (example: **a**pple)
* *Consonant-Vowel-Consonant:* taking letters, phonetically saying them out loud, and bringing the sounds together to form words.

Recommended (Age Appropriate) Reading Chunks

* Verses 1–4
* Verses 5–8
* Verses 9–11
* Verses 12–15
* Verses 16–19
* Verses 20–24

Gospel Principle Review/Activity

* What did the Lord tell Nephi's father, Lehi?
* What are some things that Nephi saw when he traveled in the wilderness?
* How did Nephi's older brothers feel about leaving Jerusalem?
* How did Nephi feel about what his father, Lehi, said? Did he trust his words?
* *Activity:* As a family, play the "what if" game. Ask each other, "What if you had to leave your home? What would you bring on the trip and why?"

Word Patterns

am

Lesson 2: words made with –am word pattern.
Use alphabet letters to create words.

1 Nephi 2

1 For behold, it came to pass that the Lord spake unto my father, yea, even in a dream, and said unto him: Blessed art thou Lehi, because of the things which thou hast done; and because thou hast been faithful and declared unto this people the things which I commanded thee, behold, they seek to take away thy life.

2 And it came to pass that the Lord commanded my father, even in a dream, that he should take his family and depart into the wilderness.

3 And it came to pass that he was obedient unto the word of the Lord, wherefore he did as the Lord commanded him.

4 And it came to pass that he departed into the wilderness. And he left his house, and the land of his inheritance, and his gold, and his silver, and his precious things, and took nothing with him, save it were his family, and provisions, and tents, and departed into the wilderness.

5 And he came down by the borders near the shore of the Red Sea; and he traveled in the wilderness in the borders which are nearer the Red Sea; and he did travel in the wilderness with his family, which consisted of my mother, Sariah, and my elder brothers, who were Laman, Lemuel, and Sam.

6 And it came to pass that when he had traveled three days in the wilderness, he pitched his tent in a valley by the side of a river of water.

7 And it came to pass that he built an altar of stones, and made an offering unto the Lord, and gave thanks unto the Lord our God.

8 And it came to pass that he called the name of the river, Laman, and it emptied into the Red Sea; and the valley was in the borders near the mouth thereof.

9 And when my father saw that the waters of the river emptied into the fountain of the Red Sea, he spake unto Laman, saying: O that thou mightest be like unto this river, continually running into the fountain of all righteousness!

10 And he also spake unto Lemuel: O that thou mightest be like unto this valley, firm and steadfast, and immovable in keeping the commandments of the Lord!

11 Now this he spake because of the stiffneckedness of Laman and Lemuel; for behold they did murmur in many things against their father, because he was a visionary man, and had led them out of the land of Jerusalem, to leave the land of their inheritance, and their gold, and their silver, and their precious things, to perish in the wilderness. And this they said he had done because of the foolish imaginations of his heart.

Date _____
☐ Completed

Date _____
☐ Completed

Date _____
☐ Completed

12 And thus Laman and Lemuel, being the eldest, did murmur against their father. And they did murmur because they knew not the dealings of that God who had created them.

13 Neither did they believe that Jerusalem, that great city, could be destroyed according to the words of the prophets. And they were like unto the Jews who were at Jerusalem, who sought to take away the life of my father.

14 And it came to pass that my father did speak unto them in the valley of Lemuel, with power, being filled with the Spirit, until their frames did shake before him. And he did confound them, that they durst not utter against him; wherefore, they did as he commanded them.

15 And my father dwelt in a tent.

16 And it came to pass that I, Nephi, being exceedingly young, nevertheless being large in stature, and also having great desires to know of the mysteries of God, wherefore, I did cry unto the Lord; and behold he did visit me, and did soften my heart that I did believe all the words which had been spoken by my father; wherefore, I did not rebel against him like unto my brothers.

17 And I spake unto Sam, making known unto him the things which the Lord had manifested unto me by his Holy Spirit. And it came to pass that he believed in my words.

18 But, behold, Laman and Lemuel would not hearken unto my words; and being grieved because of the hardness of their hearts I cried unto the Lord for them.

19 And it came to pass that the Lord spake unto me, saying: Blessed art thou, Nephi, because of thy faith, for thou hast sought me diligently, with lowliness of heart.

20 And inasmuch as ye shall keep my commandments, ye shall prosper, and shall be led to a land of promise; yea, even a land which I have prepared for you; yea, a land which is choice above all other lands.

21 And inasmuch as thy brethren shall rebel against thee, they shall be cut off from the presence of the Lord.

22 And inasmuch as thou shalt keep my commandments, thou shalt be made a ruler and a teacher over thy brethren.

23 For behold, in that day that they shall rebel against me, I will curse them even with a sore curse, and they shall have no power over thy seed except they shall rebel against me also.

24 And if it so be that they rebel against me, they shall be a scourge unto thy seed, to stir them up in the ways of remembrance.

Date _____
☐ Completed

Date _____
☐ Completed

Date _____
☐ Completed

1 Nephi

Chapter 3

Sight (Memorization) Words

go	do

Word Pattern

Pattern	-at
Pattern words in scriptures	**that, sat**
Location in chapter	Verses 1,2, 4, 7, 8, 10, 11, 13, 15, 17–20
Exceptions to the rule	"What" doesn't make the short A sound.
Other words made from this pattern not found in chapter	bat, cat, fat, hat mat, pat, rat spat, stat

Phonics Application

- *Short vowel sounds:* the sound of the letter phonetically (versus the long sound or name of the letter).
  - The short sound of A (example: **a**pple)
- *Consonant-Vowel-Consonant:* taking letters, phonetically saying them out loud, and bringing the sounds together to form words.
- *Blend-Vowel-Consonant:* a blend is the combination of two (or more) consonants together. These are the blends: BL, CL, FL, GL, PL, SL, BR, CR, DR, FR, GR, PR, TR, SC, SK, SM, SN, SP, ST, SW, TW.
- *Consonant Diagraph:* diagraphs are two letters that make one sound.
  - *"TH" sound*—makes two sounds, for example: 1) the, 2) forth

Recommended (Age Appropriate) Reading Chunks

- Verses 1–4
- Verses 5–8
- Verses 9–13
- Verses 14–17
- Verses 18–21
- Verses 22–25
- Verses 26–28
- Verses 29–31

Gospel Principle Review/Activity

- What would you have done to get the plates from Laban? What did Nephi do to get the plates?
- *Activity:* In olden days, people used to "cast lots" to decide who was chosen to do something. Play the same game.
  - Gather sticks (or similar items) and cut them into varying lengths.
  - Hold them so that you cannot tell which one is the shortest, and have everyone draw a "lot."
  - The person with the shortest lot loses.

Word Patterns

___at

Lesson 3: words made with –at word pattern.
Use alphabet letters to create words.

1 Nephi 3

1 And it came to pass that I, Nephi, returned from speaking with the Lord, to the tent of my father.

2 And it came to pass that he spake unto me, saying: Behold I have dreamed a dream, in the which the Lord hath commanded me that thou and thy brethren shall return to Jerusalem.

3 For behold, Laban hath the record of the Jews and also a genealogy of my forefathers, and they are engraven upon plates of brass.

4 Wherefore, the Lord hath commanded me that thou and thy brothers should go unto the house of Laban, and seek the records, and bring them down hither into the wilderness.

5 And now, behold thy brothers murmur, saying it is a hard thing which I have required of them; but behold I have not required it of them, but it is a commandment of the Lord.

6 Therefore go, my son, and thou shalt be favored of the Lord, because thou hast not murmured.

7 And it came to pass that I, Nephi, said unto my father: I will go and do the things which the Lord hath commanded, for I know that the Lord giveth no commandments unto the children of men, save he shall prepare a way for them that they may accomplish the thing which he commandeth them.

8 And it came to pass that when my father had heard these words he was exceedingly glad, for he knew that I had been blessed of the Lord.

9 And I, Nephi, and my brethren took our journey in the wilderness, with our tents, to go up to the land of Jerusalem.

10 And it came to pass that when we had gone up to the land of Jerusalem, I and my brethren did consult one with another.

11 And we cast lots—who of us should go in unto the house of Laban. And it came to pass that the lot fell upon Laman; and Laman went in unto the house of Laban, and he talked with him as he sat in his house.

12 And he desired of Laban the records which were engraven upon the plates of brass, which contained the genealogy of my father.

13 And behold, it came to pass that Laban was angry, and thrust him out from his presence; and he would not that he should have the records. Wherefore, he said unto him: Behold thou art a robber, and I will slay thee.

14 But Laman fled out of his presence, and told the things which Laban had done, unto us. And we began to be exceedingly sorrowful, and my brethren were about to return unto my father in the wilderness.

Date _____
☐ Completed

Date _____
☐ Completed

Date _____
☐ Completed

15 But behold I said unto them that: As the Lord liveth, and as we live, we will not go down unto our father in the wilderness until we have accomplished the thing which the Lord hath commanded us.

16 Wherefore, let us be faithful in keeping the commandments of the Lord; therefore let us go down to the land of our father's inheritance, for behold he left gold and silver, and all manner of riches. And all this he hath done because of the commandments of the Lord.

17 For he knew that Jerusalem must be destroyed, because of the wickedness of the people.

18 For behold, they have rejected the words of the prophets. Wherefore, if my father should dwell in the land after he hath been commanded to flee out of the land, behold, he would also perish. Wherefore, it must needs be that he flee out of the land.

19 And behold, it is wisdom in God that we should obtain these records, that we may preserve unto our children the language of our fathers;

20 And also that we may preserve unto them the words which have been spoken by the mouth of all the holy prophets, which have been delivered unto them by the Spirit and power of God, since the world began, even down unto this present time.

21 And it came to pass that after this manner of language did I persuade my brethren, that they might be faithful in keeping the commandments of God.

22 And it came to pass that we went down to the land of our inheritance, and we did gather together our gold, and our silver, and our precious things.

23 And after we had gathered these things together, we went up again unto the house of Laban.

24 And it came to pass that we went in unto Laban, and desired him that he would give unto us the records which were engraven upon the plates of brass, for which we would give unto him our gold, and our silver, and all our precious things.

25 And it came to pass that when Laban saw our property, and that it was exceedingly great, he did lust after it, insomuch that he thrust us out, and sent his servants to slay us, that he might obtain our property.

26 And it came to pass that we did flee before the servants of Laban, and we were obliged to leave behind our property, and it fell into the hands of Laban.

27 And it came to pass that we fled into the wilderness, and the servants of Laban did not overtake us, and we hid ourselves in the cavity of a rock.

28 And it came to pass that Laman was angry with me, and also with my father; and also was Lemuel, for he hearkened unto the words of Laman. Wherefore Laman and Lemuel did speak many hard words unto us, their younger brothers, and they did smite us even with a rod.

Notes

Date _____
☐ Completed

Date _____
☐ Completed

Date _____
☐ Completed

Date _____
☐ Completed

29 And it came to pass as they smote us with a rod, behold, an angel of the Lord came and stood before them, and he spake unto them, saying: Why do ye smite your younger brother with a rod? Know ye not that the Lord hath chosen him to be a ruler over you, and this because of your iniquities? Behold ye shall go up to Jerusalem again, and the Lord will deliver Laban into your hands.

30 And after the angel had spoken unto us, he departed.

31 And after the angel had departed, Laman and Lemuel again began to murmur, saying: How is it possible that the Lord will deliver Laban into our hands? Behold, he is a mighty man, and he can command fifty, yea, even he can slay fifty; then why not us?

Date _____

☐ Completed

1 Nephi

Chapter 4

Sight (Memorization) Words

yea

Word Pattern

Pattern	-an
Pattern words in scriptures	**than, an, can, man**
Location in chapter	Verses 1, 3, 7, 10, 13, 31, 33, 35, 37
Other words made from this patterns not found in chapter	ban, Dan, fan, Jan, pan, ran, van, clan, plan, Fran, scan, Stan

Phonics Application

- *Short vowel sounds:* the sound of the letter phonetically (versus the long sound or name of the letter).
  - The short sound of A (example: **a**pple)
- *Consonant-Vowel-Consonant:* taking letters, phonetically saying them out loud, and bringing the sounds together to form words.
- *Blend-Vowel-Consonant:* a blend is the combination of two (or more) consonants together. The blends are BL, CL, FL, GL, PL, SL, BR, CR, DR, FR, GR, PR, TR, SC, SK, SM, SN, SP, ST, SW, TW.
- *Consonant Diagraph:* diagraphs are two letters that make one sound.
  - *"CH" sound*—for example: **ch**ip

Recommended (Age Appropriate) Reading Chunks

- Verses 1–3
- Verses 4–7
- Verses 8–11
- Verses 12–15
- Verses 16–20
- Verses 21–26
- Verses 27–30
- Verses 31–34
- Verses 35–38

Gospel Principle Review/Activity

- What is the difference between obeying the commandments and obeying the direction the Spirit gives us?
- *Activity:* Blindfold the student. Tell the student which way to go to get across the room (you can add obstacles if desired).
  - Why was it important to listen to your parent?
  - How is this like the Spirit?

Word Patterns

an

Lesson 4: words made with –an word pattern.
Use alphabet letters to create words.

1 Nephi 4

1 And it came to pass that I spake unto my brethren, saying: Let us go up again unto Jerusalem, and let us be faithful in keeping the commandments of the Lord; for behold he is mightier than all the earth, then why not mightier than Laban and his fifty, yea, or even than his tens of thousands?

2 Therefore let us go up; let us be strong like unto Moses; for he truly spake unto the waters of the Red Sea and they divided hither and thither, and our fathers came through, out of captivity, on dry ground, and the armies of Pharaoh did follow and were drowned in the waters of the Red Sea.

3 Now behold ye know that this is true; and ye also know that an angel hath spoken unto you; wherefore can ye doubt? Let us go up; the Lord is able to deliver us, even as our fathers, and to destroy Laban, even as the Egyptians.

4 Now when I had spoken these words, they were yet wroth, and did still continue to murmur; nevertheless they did follow me up until we came without the walls of Jerusalem.

5 And it was by night; and I caused that they should hide themselves without the walls. And after they had hid themselves, I, Nephi, crept into the city and went forth towards the house of Laban.

6 And I was led by the Spirit, not knowing beforehand the things which I should do.

7 Nevertheless I went forth, and as I came near unto the house of Laban I beheld a man, and he had fallen to the earth before me, for he was drunken with wine.

8 And when I came to him I found that it was Laban.

9 And I beheld his sword, and I drew it forth from the sheath thereof; and the hilt thereof was of pure gold, and the workmanship thereof was exceedingly fine, and I saw that the blade thereof was of the most precious steel.

10 And it came to pass that I was constrained by the Spirit that I should kill Laban; but I said in my heart: Never at any time have I shed the blood of man. And I shrunk and would that I might not slay him.

11 And the Spirit said unto me again: Behold the Lord hath delivered him into thy hands. Yea, and I also knew that he had sought to take away mine own life; yea, and he would not hearken unto the commandments of the Lord; and he also had taken away our property.

Date _____
☐ Completed

Date _____
☐ Completed

Date _____
☐ Completed

12 And it came to pass that the Spirit said unto me again: Slay him, for the Lord hath delivered him into thy hands;

13 Behold the Lord slayeth the wicked to bring forth his righteous purposes. It is better that one man should perish than that a nation should dwindle and perish in unbelief.

14 And now, when I, Nephi, had heard these words, I remembered the words of the Lord which he spake unto me in the wilderness, saying that: Inasmuch as thy seed shall keep my commandments, they shall prosper in the land of promise.

15 Yea, and I also thought that they could not keep the commandments of the Lord according to the law of Moses, save they should have the law.

16 And I also knew that the law was engraven upon the plates of brass.

17 And again, I knew that the Lord had delivered Laban into my hands for this cause—that I might obtain the records according to his commandments.

18 Therefore I did obey the voice of the Spirit, and took Laban by the hair of the head, and I smote off his head with his own sword.

19 And after I had smitten off his head with his own sword, I took the garments of Laban and put them upon mine own body; yea, even every whit; and I did gird on his armor about my loins.

20 And after I had done this, I went forth unto the treasury of Laban. And as I went forth towards the treasury of Laban, behold, I saw the servant of Laban who had the keys of the treasury. And I commanded him in the voice of Laban, that he should go with me into the treasury.

21 And he supposed me to be his master, Laban, for he beheld the garments and also the sword girded about my loins.

22 And he spake unto me concerning the elders of the Jews, he knowing that his master, Laban, had been out by night among them.

23 And I spake unto him as if it had been Laban.

24 And I also spake unto him that I should carry the engravings, which were upon the plates of brass, to my elder brethren, who were without the walls.

25 And I also bade him that he should follow me.

26 And he, supposing that I spake of the brethren of the church, and that I was truly that Laban whom I had slain, wherefore he did follow me.

27 And he spake unto me many times concerning the elders of the Jews, as I went forth unto my brethren, who were without the walls.

28 And it came to pass that when Laman saw me he was exceedingly

Date _____
☐ Completed

Date _____
☐ Completed

Date _____
☐ Completed

frightened, and also Lemuel and Sam. And they fled from before my presence; for they supposed it was Laban, and that he had slain me and had sought to take away their lives also.

29 And it came to pass that I called after them, and they did hear me; wherefore they did cease to flee from my presence.

30 And it came to pass that when the servant of Laban beheld my brethren he began to tremble, and was about to flee from before me and return to the city of Jerusalem.

---

31 And now I, Nephi, being a man large in stature, and also having received much strength of the Lord, therefore I did seize upon the servant of Laban, and held him, that he should not flee.

32 And it came to pass that I spake with him, that if he would hearken unto my words, as the Lord liveth, and as I live, even so that if he would hearken unto our words, we would spare his life.

33 And I spake unto him, even with an oath, that he need not fear; that he should be a free man like unto us if he would go down in the wilderness with us.

34 And I also spake unto him, saying: Surely the Lord hath commanded us to do this thing; and shall we not be diligent in keeping the commandments of the Lord? Therefore, if thou wilt go down into the wilderness to my father thou shalt have place with us.

---

35 And it came to pass that Zoram did take courage at the words which I spake. Now Zoram was the name of the servant; and he promised that he would go down into the wilderness unto our father. Yea, and he also made an oath unto us that he would tarry with us from that time forth.

36 Now we were desirous that he should tarry with us for this cause, that the Jews might not know concerning our flight into the wilderness, lest they should pursue us and destroy us.

37 And it came to pass that when Zoram had made an oath unto us, our fears did cease concerning him.

38 And it came to pass that we took the plates of brass and the servant of Laban, and departed into the wilderness, and journeyed unto the tent of our father.

Notes

Date _____
☐ Completed

Date _____
☐ Completed

Date _____
☐ Completed

1 Nephi

Chapter 5

Sight (Memorization) Words

of

Word Pattern

Pattern	-ed
Pattern words in scriptures	**led**
Location in chapter	Verses 2, 15
Other words made from this patterns not found in chapter	bed, fed, Ned, Ted, wed, bled, fled, sled, sped, shed

Phonics Application

- *Short vowel sounds:* the sound of the letter phonetically (versus the long sound or name of the letter).
  - The short sound of E (example: b**e**d)
- *Consonant-Vowel-Consonant:* taking letters, phonetically saying them out loud, and bringing the sounds together to form words.
- *Blend-Vowel-Consonant:* a blend is the combination of two (or more) consonants together. These are the blends: BL, CL, FL, GL, PL, SL, BR, CR, DR, FR, GR, PR, TR, SC, SK, SM, SN, SP, ST, SW, TW.
- *Consonant Diagraph:* diagraphs are two letters that make one sound.
  - *"SH" sound*—for example: **sh**ip

Recommended (Age Appropriate) Reading Chunks

- Verses 1–4
- Verses 5–8
- Verses 9–12
- Verses 13–16
- Verses 17–22

Gospel Principle Review/Activity

- What would you have done if you were Sariah?
- What did Lehi do with the plates?
- *Activity:* Understand a mother's love by doing the following:
  - Reading your mother's journal entries from when you were born.
  - Having her write you a special note.
  - Having her show you your baby pictures and telling you stories.

Word Patterns

_ed

Lesson 5: words made with –ed word pattern.
Use alphabet letters to create words.

1 Nephi 5

1 And it came to pass that after we had come down into the wilderness unto our father, behold, he was filled with joy, and also my mother, Sariah, was exceedingly glad, for she truly had mourned because of us.

2 For she had supposed that we had perished in the wilderness; and she also had complained against my father, telling him that he was a visionary man; saying: Behold thou hast led us forth from the land of our inheritance, and my sons are no more, and we perish in the wilderness.

3 And after this manner of language had my mother complained against my father.

4 And it had come to pass that my father spake unto her, saying: I know that I am a visionary man; for if I had not seen the things of God in a vision I should not have known the goodness of God, but had tarried at Jerusalem, and had perished with my brethren.

Date _____
☐ Completed

5 But behold, I have obtained a land of promise, in the which things I do rejoice; yea, and I know that the Lord will deliver my sons out of the hands of Laban, and bring them down again unto us in the wilderness.

6 And after this manner of language did my father, Lehi, comfort my mother, Sariah, concerning us, while we journeyed in the wilderness up to the land of Jerusalem, to obtain the record of the Jews.

7 And when we had returned to the tent of my father, behold their joy was full, and my mother was comforted.

8 And she spake, saying: Now I know of a surety that the Lord hath commanded my husband to flee into the wilderness; yea, and I also know of a surety that the Lord hath protected my sons, and delivered them out of the hands of Laban, and given them power whereby they could accomplish the thing which the Lord hath commanded them. And after this manner of language did she speak.

Date _____
☐ Completed

9 And it came to pass that they did rejoice exceedingly, and did offer sacrifice and burnt offerings unto the Lord; and they gave thanks unto the God of Israel.

10 And after they had given thanks unto the God of Israel, my father, Lehi, took the records which were engraven upon the plates of brass, and he did search them from the beginning.

11 And he beheld that they did contain the five books of Moses, which gave an account of the creation of the world, and also of Adam and Eve, who were our first parents;

12 And also a record of the Jews from the beginning, even down to the commencement of the reign of Zedekiah, king of Judah;

Date _____
☐ Completed

13 And also the prophecies of the holy prophets, from the beginning, even down to the commencement of the reign of Zedekiah; and also many prophecies which have been spoken by the mouth of Jeremiah.

14 And it came to pass that my father, Lehi, also found upon the plates of brass a genealogy of his fathers; wherefore he knew that he was a descendant of Joseph; yea, even that Joseph who was the son of Jacob, who was sold into Egypt, and who was preserved by the hand of the Lord, that he might preserve his father, Jacob, and all his household from perishing with famine.

15 And they were also led out of captivity and out of the land of Egypt, by that same God who had preserved them.

16 And thus my father, Lehi, did discover the genealogy of his fathers. And Laban also was a descendant of Joseph, wherefore he and his fathers had kept the records.

17 And now when my father saw all these things, he was filled with the Spirit, and began to prophesy concerning his seed—

18 That these plates of brass should go forth unto all nations, kindreds, tongues, and people who were of his seed.

19 Wherefore, he said that these plates of brass should never perish; neither should they be dimmed any more by time. And he prophesied many things concerning his seed.

20 And it came to pass that thus far I and my father had kept the commandments wherewith the Lord had commanded us.

21 And we had obtained the records which the Lord had commanded us, and searched them and found that they were desirable; yea, even of great worth unto us, insomuch that we could preserve the commandments of the Lord unto our children.

22 Wherefore, it was wisdom in the Lord that we should carry them with us, as we journeyed in the wilderness towards the land of promise.

Notes

Date _____
☐ Completed

Date _____
☐ Completed

22

1 Nephi

Chapter 6

Sight (Memorization) Words

as

Word Pattern

Pattern	-en
Pattern words in scriptures	**men**
Location in chapter	Verses 4, 6
Other words made from this patterns not found in chapter	Ben, den, hen, pen, ten, glen, then, when

Phonics Application

- *Short vowel sounds:* the sound of the letter phonetically (versus the long sound or name of the letter).
  - The short sound of E (example: b**e**d)
- *Consonant-Vowel-Consonant:* taking letters, phonetically saying them out loud, and bringing the sounds together to form words.
- *Blend-Vowel-Consonant:* a blend is the combination of two (or more) consonants together. These are the blends: BL, CL, FL, GL, PL, SL, BR, CR, DR, FR, GR, PR, TR, SC, SK, SM, SN, SP, ST, SW, TW.
- *Consonant Diagraph:* diagraphs are two letters that make one sound.
  - *"WH" sound*—for example: **wh**ip

Recommended (Age Appropriate) Reading Chunks

- Verses 1–3
- Verses 4–6

Gospel Principle Review/Activity

- What is a descendant?
- *Activity:* Nephi and other prophets often told how they were descendents of famous prophets. They did this so that they could show that they had the same blood as very righteous men. Are you a descendent of any prophets, presidents, or leaders? If so, fill out the statement below.

I am a descendent of _____.

Word Patterns

__en

Lesson 6: words made with –en word pattern.
Use alphabet letters to create words.

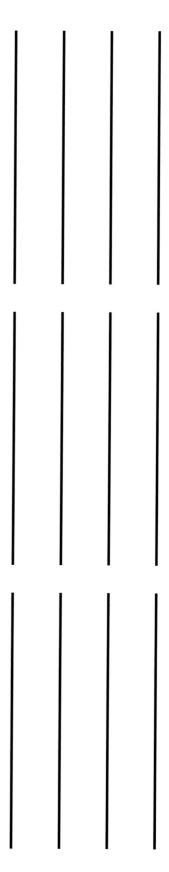

1 Nephi 6

1 And now I, Nephi, do not give the genealogy of my fathers in this part of my record; neither at any time shall I give it after upon these plates which I am writing; for it is given in the record which has been kept by my father; wherefore, I do not write it in this work.
2 For it sufficeth me to say that we are descendants of Joseph.
3 And it mattereth not to me that I am particular to give a full account of all the things of my father, for they cannot be written upon these plates, for I desire the room that I may write of the things of God.

4 For the fulness of mine intent is that I may persuade men to come unto the God of Abraham, and the God of Isaac, and the God of Jacob, and be saved.
5 Wherefore, the things which are pleasing unto the world I do not write, but the things which are pleasing unto God and unto those who are not of the world.
6 Wherefore, I shall give commandment unto my seed, that they shall not occupy these plates with things which are not of worth unto the children of men.

Date _____
☐ Completed

Date _____
☐ Completed

1 Nephi

Chapter 7

Sight (Memorization) Words

(Note: see phonics application for a pattern for this sight word.)

Word Pattern

Pattern	-et
Pattern words in scriptures	**set, let**
Location in chapter	Verses 8, 12
Other words made from this patterns not found in chapter	bet, get, met, pet, vet, wet, yet

Phonics Application

- *Words that end with vowels:* when a word ends with a vowel and it is the only vowel in the word, the vowel is usually a LONG vowel, or a vowel that says its name (example: y**e**).
- *Short vowel sounds:* the sound of the letter phonetically (versus the long sound or name of the letter).
  - The short sound of E (example: b**e**d)
- *Consonant-Vowel-Consonant:* taking letters, phonetically saying them out loud, and bringing the sounds together to form words.
- *Blend-Vowel-Consonant:* a blend is the combination of two (or more) consonants together. These are the blends: BL, CL, FL, GL, PL, SL, BR, CR, DR, FR, GR, PR, TR, SC, SK, SM, SN, SP, ST, SW, TW.
- *Consonant Diagraphs:* diagraphs are two letters that make one sound. The diagraphs are TH, CH, SH, WH.

Recommended (Age Appropriate) Reading Chunks

- Verses 1–3
- Verses 4–7
- Verses 8–12
- Verses 13–15
- Verses 16–19
- Verses 20–22

Gospel Principle Review/Activity

- Why did Nephi and his brothers have to go back to Jerusalem again?
- Who did they bring back with them?
- *Activity:* Nephi had a hard time agreeing with his brothers. What are some ways that you can overcome arguments with your brothers and sisters? Make a list and try one new idea this week.

Word Patterns

___ et

Lesson 7: words made with –et word pattern.
Use alphabet letters to recreate words.

1 Nephi 7

1 And now I would that ye might know, that after my father, Lehi, had made an end of prophesying concerning his seed, it came to pass that the Lord spake unto him again, saying that it was not meet for him, Lehi, that he should take his family into the wilderness alone; but that his sons should take daughters to wife, that they might raise up seed unto the Lord in the land of promise.

2 And it came to pass that the Lord commanded him that I, Nephi, and my brethren, should again return unto the land of Jerusalem, and bring down Ishmael and his family into the wilderness.

3 And it came to pass that I, Nephi, did again, with my brethren, go forth into the wilderness to go up to Jerusalem.

4 And it came to pass that we went up unto the house of Ishmael, and we did gain favor in the sight of Ishmael, insomuch that we did speak unto him the words of the Lord.

5 And it came to pass that the Lord did soften the heart of Ishmael, and also his household, insomuch that they took their journey with us down into the wilderness to the tent of our father.

6 And it came to pass that as we journeyed in the wilderness, behold Laman and Lemuel, and two of the daughters of Ishmael, and the two sons of Ishmael and their families, did rebel against us; yea, against me, Nephi, and Sam, and their father, Ishmael, and his wife, and his three other daughters.

7 And it came to pass in the which rebellion, they were desirous to return unto the land of Jerusalem.

8 And now I, Nephi, being grieved for the hardness of their hearts, therefore I spake unto them, saying, yea, even unto Laman and unto Lemuel: Behold ye are mine elder brethren, and how is it that ye are so hard in your hearts, and so blind in your minds, that ye have need that I, your younger brother, should speak unto you, yea, and set an example for you?

9 How is it that ye have not hearkened unto the word of the Lord?

10 How is it that ye have forgotten that ye have seen an angel of the Lord?

11 Yea, and how is it that ye have forgotten what great things the Lord hath done for us, in delivering us out of the hands of Laban, and also that we should obtain the record?

12 Yea, and how is it that ye have forgotten that the Lord is able to do all things according to his will, for the children of men, if it so be that they exercise faith in him? Wherefore, let us be faithful to him.

Date _____
☐ Completed

Date _____
☐ Completed

Date _____
☐ Completed

13 And if it so be that we are faithful to him, we shall obtain the land of promise; and ye shall know at some future period that the word of the Lord shall be fulfilled concerning the destruction of Jerusalem; for all things which the Lord hath spoken concerning the destruction of Jerusalem must be fulfilled.

14 For behold, the Spirit of the Lord ceaseth soon to strive with them; for behold, they have rejected the prophets, and Jeremiah have they cast into prison. And they have sought to take away the life of my father, insomuch that they have driven him out of the land.

15 Now behold, I say unto you that if ye will return unto Jerusalem ye shall also perish with them. And now, if ye have choice, go up to the land, and remember the words which I speak unto you, that if ye go ye will also perish; for thus the Spirit of the Lord constraineth me that I should speak.

16 And it came to pass that when I, Nephi, had spoken these words unto my brethren, they were angry with me. And it came to pass that they did lay their hands upon me, for behold, they were exceedingly wroth, and they did bind me with cords, for they sought to take away my life, that they might leave me in the wilderness to be devoured by wild beasts.

17 But it came to pass that I prayed unto the Lord, saying: O Lord, according to my faith which is in thee, wilt thou deliver me from the hands of my brethren; yea, even give me strength that I may burst these bands with which I am bound.

18 And it came to pass that when I had said these words, behold, the bands were loosed from off my hands and feet, and I stood before my brethren, and I spake unto them again.

19 And it came to pass that they were angry with me again, and sought to lay hands upon me; but behold, one of the daughters of Ishmael, yea, and also her mother, and one of the sons of Ishmael, did plead with my brethren, insomuch that they did soften their hearts; and they did cease striving to take away my life.

20 And it came to pass that they were sorrowful, because of their wickedness, insomuch that they did bow down before me, and did plead with me that I would forgive them of the thing that they had done against me.

21 And it came to pass that I did frankly forgive them all that they had done, and I did exhort them that they would pray unto the Lord their God for forgiveness. And it came to pass that they did so. And after they had done praying unto the Lord we did again travel on our journey towards the tent of our father.

22 And it came to pass that we did come down unto the tent of our father. And after I and my brethren and all the house of Ishmael had come down unto the tent of my father, they did give thanks unto the Lord their God; and they did offer sacrifice and burnt offerings unto him.

Notes

_____
_____
_____
_____
_____
_____
_____
_____
_____

Date _____
☐ Completed

_____
_____
_____
_____
_____
_____
_____
_____
_____
_____

Date _____
☐ Completed

_____
_____
_____
_____
_____
_____

Date _____
☐ Completed

29

1 Nephi

Chapter 8

Sight (Memorization) Words

or

(Note: the -or pattern is related to the R-controlled vowels explained in Mosiah 13.)

Word Pattern

Pattern	-in
Pattern words in scriptures	**in**
Location in chapter	Verses 2–5, 7–8, 22–23, 26–27, 30, 32, 36
Other words made from this patterns not found in chapter	fin, kin, pin, sin, bin, tin, win, grin, skin, spin, twin, chin, shin, thin

Phonics Application

- *Short vowel sounds:* the sound of the letter phonetically (versus the long sound or name of the letter).
  - The short sound of I (example: h**i**t)
- *Consonant-Vowel-Consonant:* taking letters, phonetically saying them out loud, and bringing the sounds together to form words.
- *Blend-Vowel-Consonant:* a blend is the combination of two (or more) consonants together. These are the blends: BL, CL, FL, GL, PL, SL, BR, CR, DR, FR, GR, PR, TR, SC, SK, SM, SN, SP, ST, SW, TW.
- *Consonant Diagraphs:* diagraphs are two letters that make one sound. The diagraphs are TH, CH, SH, WH.
- *Complex Consonants:* blends that include three consonants, two consonants that sound like a single letter, and consonant and vowel clusters.
  - *Lazy Q*—Q is always with U. The U is silent (example: queen, quilt, quiet).

Recommended (Age Appropriate) Reading Chunks

- Verses 1–4
- Verses 5–9
- Verses 10–13
- Verses 14–18
- Verses 19–23
- Verses 24–27
- Verses 28–33
- Verses 34–38

Gospel Principle Review/Activity

- What is a vision? What is the difference between a vision and a dream?
- Who do you think it was that was dressed in a white robe?
- What does the "rod of iron" represent?
- *Activity:* Draw a picture of what you think Lehi's vision looked like. Have a parent read the description again as you draw.

Word Patterns

_in

Lesson 8: words made with –in word pattern.
Use alphabet letters to create words.

1 Nephi 8

1 And it came to pass that we had gathered together all manner of seeds of every kind, both of grain of every kind, and also of the seeds of fruit of every kind.

2 And it came to pass that while my father tarried in the wilderness he spake unto us, saying: Behold, I have dreamed a dream; or, in other words, I have seen a vision.

3 And behold, because of the thing which I have seen, I have reason to rejoice in the Lord because of Nephi and also of Sam; for I have reason to suppose that they, and also many of their seed, will be saved.

4 But behold, Laman and Lemuel, I fear exceedingly because of you; for behold, methought I saw in my dream, a dark and dreary wilderness.

---

5 And it came to pass that I saw a man, and he was dressed in a white robe; and he came and stood before me.

6 And it came to pass that he spake unto me, and bade me follow him.

7 And it came to pass that as I followed him I beheld myself that I was in a dark and dreary waste.

8 And after I had traveled for the space of many hours in darkness, I began to pray unto the Lord that he would have mercy on me, according to the multitude of his tender mercies.

9 And it came to pass after I had prayed unto the Lord I beheld a large and spacious field.

---

10 And it came to pass that I beheld a tree, whose fruit was desirable to make one happy.

11 And it came to pass that I did go forth and partake of the fruit thereof; and I beheld that it was most sweet, above all that I ever before tasted. Yea, and I beheld that the fruit thereof was white, to exceed all the whiteness that I had ever seen.

12 And as I partook of the fruit thereof it filled my soul with exceedingly great joy; wherefore, I began to be desirous that my family should partake of it also; for I knew that it was desirable above all other fruit.

13 And as I cast my eyes round about, that perhaps I might discover my family also, I beheld a river of water; and it ran along, and it was near the tree of which I was partaking the fruit.

---

14 And I looked to behold from whence it came; and I saw the head thereof a little way off; and at the head thereof I beheld your mother Sariah, and Sam, and Nephi; and they stood as if they knew not whither they should go.

Date _____
☐ Completed

Date _____
☐ Completed

Date _____
☐ Completed

15 And it came to pass that I beckoned unto them; and I also did say unto them with a loud voice that they should come unto me, and partake of the fruit, which was desirable above all other fruit.

16 And it came to pass that they did come unto me and partake of the fruit also.

17 And it came to pass that I was desirous that Laman and Lemuel should come and partake of the fruit also; wherefore, I cast mine eyes towards the head of the river, that perhaps I might see them.

18 And it came to pass that I saw them, but they would not come unto me and partake of the fruit.

19 And I beheld a rod of iron, and it extended along the bank of the river, and led to the tree by which I stood.

20 And I also beheld a strait and narrow path, which came along by the rod of iron, even to the tree by which I stood; and it also led by the head of the fountain, unto a large and spacious field, as if it had been a world.

21 And I saw numberless concourses of people, many of whom were pressing forward, that they might obtain the path which led unto the tree by which I stood.

22 And it came to pass that they did come forth, and commence in the path which led to the tree.

23 And it came to pass that there arose a mist of darkness; yea, even an exceedingly great mist of darkness, insomuch that they who had commenced in the path did lose their way, that they wandered off and were lost.

24 And it came to pass that I beheld others pressing forward, and they came forth and caught hold of the end of the rod of iron; and they did press forward through the mist of darkness, clinging to the rod of iron, even until they did come forth and partake of the fruit of the tree.

25 And after they had partaken of the fruit of the tree they did cast their eyes about as if they were ashamed.

26 And I also cast my eyes round about, and beheld, on the other side of the river of water, a great and spacious building; and it stood as it were in the air, high above the earth.

27 And it was filled with people, both old and young, both male and female; and their manner of dress was exceedingly fine; and they were in the attitude of mocking and pointing their fingers towards those who had come at and were partaking of the fruit.

28 And after they had tasted of the fruit they were ashamed, because of those that were scoffing at them; and they fell away into forbidden paths and were lost.

29 And now I, Nephi, do not speak all the words of my father.

Notes

Date _____
☐ Completed

Date _____
☐ Completed

Date _____
☐ Completed

30 But, to be short in writing, behold, he saw other multitudes pressing forward; and they came and caught hold of the end of the rod of iron; and they did press their way forward, continually holding fast to the rod of iron, until they came forth and fell down and partook of the fruit of the tree.

31 And he also saw other multitudes feeling their way towards that great and spacious building.

32 And it came to pass that many were drowned in the depths of the fountain; and many were lost from his view, wandering in strange roads.

33 And great was the multitude that did enter into that strange building.

And after they did enter into that building they did point the finger of scorn at me and those that were partaking of the fruit also; but we heeded them not.

34 These are the words of my father: For as many as heeded them, had fallen away.

35 And Laman and Lemuel partook not of the fruit, said my father.

36 And it came to pass after my father had spoken all the words of his dream or vision, which were many, he said unto us, because of these things which he saw in a vision, he exceedingly feared for Laman and Lemuel; yea, he feared lest they should be cast off from the presence of the Lord.

37 And he did exhort them then with all the feeling of a tender parent, that they would hearken to his words, that perhaps the Lord would be merciful to them, and not cast them off; yea, my father did preach unto them.

38 And after he had preached unto them, and also prophesied unto them of many things, he bade them to keep the commandments of the Lord; and he did cease speaking unto them.

Notes

Date _____
☐ Completed

Date _____
☐ Completed

1 Nephi

Chapter 9—Review

Sight (Memorization) Words

I	a	O	the	go	do
yea	of	as	ye	or	

Word Pattern

Pattern	-ad	-am	-at	-an
Pattern words reviewed	had	Sam	that, sat	than, an can, man

Pattern	-ed	-en	-et	-in
Pattern words reviewed	led	men	set, let	in

Phonics Application

- *Short vowel sounds*: the sound of the letter phonetically (versus the long sound or name of the letter).
  - The short sound of A (example: **a**pple)
  - The short sound of E (example: b**e**d)
  - The short sound of I (example: h**i**t)
- *Consonant-Vowel-Consonant*: taking letters, phonetically saying them out loud, and bringing the sounds together to form words.
- *Blend-Vowel-Consonant*: a blend is the the combination of two (or more) consonants together. These are the blends: BL, CL, FL, GL, PL, SL, BR, CR, DR, FR, GR, PR, TR, SC, SK, SM, SN, SP, ST, SW, TW.
- *Consonant Diagraph*: diagraphs are two letters that make one sound.
  - *"TH" sound*—makes two sounds, for example: 1) the, 2) forth
  - *"CH" sound*—for example: **ch**ip
  - *"SH" sound*—for example: **sh**ip
  - *"WH" sound*—for example: **wh**ip
- *Complex Consonant*: blends that include three consonants, two consonants that sound like a single letter, and consonant and vowel clusters.
  - *Lazy Q*—Q is always with U. The U is silent (example: queen, quilt, quiet).

Recommended (Age Appropriate) Reading Chunks

- Verses 1–3
- Verses 4–6

Gospel Principle Review/Activity

- What was Nephi commanded to do?
- *Activity:* What is a "history" of a people (as Nephi talks about)? What is your family history? Where does your family come from? Make a four-generation chart.

Word Patterns—Review

Lesson 9 Review: Find the words in the word box in the word search.

L	D	Q	E	R	L	K	W
T	A	Z	V	D	A	C	I
N	H	T	P	T	U	M	N
V	E	T	S	P	A	N	E
M	S	H	N	E	B	C	J
N	E	V	Z	Y	O	P	I
D	G	C	T	U	J	F	E
K	A	B	L	K	Z	Q	R

Word Box

Ben
cat
had
met
pan
ram
shed
win

1 Nephi 9

1 And all these things did my father see, and hear, and speak, as he dwelt in a tent, in the valley of Lemuel, and also a great many more things, which cannot be written upon these plates.

2 And now, as I have spoken concerning these plates, behold they are not the plates upon which I make a full account of the history of my people; for the plates upon which I make a full account of my people I have given the name of Nephi; wherefore, they are called the plates of Nephi, after mine own name; and these plates also are called the plates of Nephi.

3 Nevertheless, I have received a commandment of the Lord that I should make these plates, for the special purpose that there should be an account engraven of the ministry of my people.

4 Upon the other plates should be engraven an account of the reign of the kings, and the wars and contentions of my people; wherefore these plates are for the more part of the ministry; and the other plates are for the more part of the reign of the kings and the wars and contentions of my people.

5 Wherefore, the Lord hath commanded me to make these plates for a wise purpose in him, which purpose I know not.

6 But the Lord knoweth all things from the beginning; wherefore, he prepareth a way to accomplish all his works among the children of men; for behold, he hath all power unto the fulfilling of all his words. And thus it is. Amen.

Date _____
☐ Completed

Date _____
☐ Completed

1 Nephi

Chapter 10

Sight (Memorization) Words

my	is

Word Pattern

Pattern	-is
Pattern words in scriptures	**this**
Location in chapter	Verses 2, 5, 6, 8, 15, 17–19
Exceptions to the rule	is and his both have the Z sound at the end (and are sight words)
Other words made from this patterns not found in chapter	(none listed)

Phonics Application

- *Words that end with vowels:* when a word ends with a vowel and it is the only vowel in the word, the vowel is usually a LONG vowel, or a vowel that says its name (example: m**y**).
- *Short vowel sounds:* the sound of the letter phonetically (versus the long sound or name of the letter).
  - The short sound of I (example: h**i**t)
- *Consonant-Vowel-Consonant:* taking letters, phonetically saying them out loud, and bringing the sounds together to form words.
- *Blend-Vowel-Consonant:* a blend is the combination of two (or more) consonants together. These are the blends: BL, CL, FL, GL, PL, SL, BR, CR, DR, FR, GR, PR, TR, SC, SK, SM, SN, SP, ST, SW, TW.
- *Consonant Diagraphs:* diagraphs are two letters that make one sound. The diagraphs are TH, CH, SH, WH.
- *Complex Consonants:* blends that include three consonants, two consonants that sounds like a single letter, and consonant and vowel clusters. The Complex Consonants are QU.

Recommended (Age Appropriate) Reading Chunks

- Verses 1–3
- Verses 4–7
- Verses 8–10
- Verses 11–13
- Verses 14–16
- Verses 17–18
- Verses 19–22

Gospel Principle Review/Activity

- What is an olive tree? What does it do?
- What is the Holy Ghost? How does it help us?
- *Activity*: To illustrate seeking and finding (verse 19), place a game of hide-and-go-seek.

Word Patterns

is

Lesson 10: words made with –is word pattern.
Use alphabet letters to create words.

1 Nephi 10

1 And now I, Nephi, proceed to give an account upon these plates of my proceedings, and my reign and ministry; wherefore, to proceed with mine account, I must speak somewhat of the things of my father, and also of my brethren.

2 For behold, it came to pass after my father had made an end of speaking the words of his dream, and also of exhorting them to all diligence, he spake unto them concerning the Jews—

3 That after they should be destroyed, even that great city Jerusalem, and many be carried away captive into Babylon, according to the own due time of the Lord, they should return again, yea, even be brought back out of captivity; and after they should be brought back out of captivity they should possess again the land of their inheritance.

4 Yea, even six hundred years from the time that my father left Jerusalem, a prophet would the Lord God raise up among the Jews—even a Messiah, or, in other words, a Savior of the world.

5 And he also spake concerning the prophets, how great a number had testified of these things, concerning this Messiah, of whom he had spoken, or this Redeemer of the world.

6 Wherefore, all mankind were in a lost and in a fallen state, and ever would be save they should rely on this Redeemer.

7 And he spake also concerning a prophet who should come before the Messiah, to prepare the way of the Lord—

8 Yea, even he should go forth and cry in the wilderness: Prepare ye the way of the Lord, and make his paths straight; for there standeth one among you whom ye know not; and he is mightier than I, whose shoe's latchet I am not worthy to unloose. And much spake my father concerning this thing.

9 And my father said he should baptize in Bethabara, beyond Jordan; and he also said he should baptize with water; even that he should baptize the Messiah with water.

10 And after he had baptized the Messiah with water, he should behold and bear record that he had baptized the Lamb of God, who should take away the sins of the world.

11 And it came to pass after my father had spoken these words he spake unto my brethren concerning the gospel which should be preached among the Jews, and also concerning the dwindling of the Jews in unbelief. And after they had slain the Messiah, who should come, and after he had been slain he should rise from the dead, and should make himself

Date _____
☐ Completed

Date _____
☐ Completed

Date _____
☐ Completed

manifest, by the Holy Ghost, unto the Gentiles.

12 Yea, even my father spake much concerning the Gentiles, and also concerning the house of Israel, that they should be compared like unto an olive-tree, whose branches should be broken off and should be scattered upon all the face of the earth.

13 Wherefore, he said it must needs be that we should be led with one accord into the land of promise, unto the fulfilling of the word of the Lord, that we should be scattered upon all the face of the earth.

14 And after the house of Israel should be scattered they should be gathered together again; or, in fine, after the Gentiles had received the fulness of the Gospel, the natural branches of the olive-tree, or the remnants of the house of Israel, should be grafted in, or come to the knowledge of the true Messiah, their Lord and their Redeemer.

15 And after this manner of language did my father prophesy and speak unto my brethren, and also many more things which I do not write in this book; for I have written as many of them as were expedient for me in mine other book.

16 And all these things, of which I have spoken, were done as my father dwelt in a tent, in the valley of Lemuel.

17 And it came to pass after I, Nephi, having heard all the words of my father, concerning the things which he saw in a vision, and also the things which he spake by the power of the Holy Ghost, which power he received by faith on the Son of God—and the Son of God was the Messiah who should come—I, Nephi, was desirous also that I might see, and hear, and know of these things, by the power of the Holy Ghost, which is the gift of God unto all those who diligently seek him, as well in times of old as in the time that he should manifest himself unto the children of men.

18 For he is the same yesterday, to-day, and forever; and the way is prepared for all men from the foundation of the world, if it so be that they repent and come unto him.

19 For he that diligently seeketh shall find; and the mysteries of God shall be unfolded unto them, by the power of the Holy Ghost, as well in these times as in times of old, and as well in times of old as in times to come; wherefore, the course of the Lord is one eternal round.

20 Therefore remember, O man, for all thy doings thou shalt be brought into judgment.

21 Wherefore, if ye have sought to do wickedly in the days of your probation, then ye are found unclean before the judgment–seat of God; and no unclean thing can dwell with God; wherefore, ye must be cast off forever.

22 And the Holy Ghost giveth authority that I should speak these things, and deny them not.

Notes

Date _____
☐ Completed

Date _____
☐ Completed

Date _____
☐ Completed

Date _____
☐ Completed

1 Nephi

Chapter 11

Sight (Memorization) Words

he	his

(Note: see phonics application for a pattern for this sight word.)

Word Pattern

Pattern	-im
Pattern words in scriptures	**Him**
Location in chapter	Verses 7, 11–12, 15, 17, 22, 24, 27–29
Other words made from this patterns not found in chapter	dim, Kim, rim, Tim, grim, trim, swim, whim

Phonics Application

- *Words that end with vowels:* when a word ends with a vowel and it is the only vowel in the word, the vowel is usually a LONG vowel, or a vowel that says its name (example: he).
- *Short vowel sounds:* the sound of the letter phonetically (versus the long sound or name of the letter).
  - The short sound of I (example: h**i**t)
- *Consonant-Vowel-Consonant:* taking letters, phonetically saying them out loud, and bringing the sounds together to form words.
- *Blend-Vowel-Consonant:* a blend is the combination of two (or more) consonants together. These are the blends: BL, CL, FL, GL, PL, SL, BR, CR, DR, FR, GR, PR, TR, SC, SK, SM, SN, SP, ST, SW, TW.
- *Consonant Diagraphs:* diagraphs are two letters that make one sound. The diagraphs are TH, CH, SH, WH.
- *Complex Consonant:* blends that include three consonants, two consonants that sounds like a single letter, and consonant and vowel clusters. The complex consonants are QU.

Recommended (Age Appropriate) Reading Chunks

- Verses 1–5
- Verses 6–8
- Verses 9–13
- Verses 14–19
- Verses 20–24
- Verses 25–28
- Verses 29–31
- Verses 32–34
- Verses 35–36

Gospel Principle Review/Activity

- Why did the Spirit ask Nephi questions?
- *Activity:* Draw a picture of what you think the "tree of life" looks like.

Word Patterns

_im

Lesson 11: words made with –im word pattern.
Use alphabet letters to create words.

1 Nephi 11

1 For it came to pass after I had desired to know the things that my father had seen, and believing that the Lord was able to make them known unto me, as I sat pondering in mine heart I was caught away in the Spirit of the Lord, yea, into an exceedingly high mountain, which I never had before seen, and upon which I never had before set my foot.

2 And the Spirit said unto me: Behold, what desirest thou?

3 And I said: I desire to behold the things which my father saw.

4 And the Spirit said unto me: Believest thou that thy father saw the tree of which he hath spoken?

5 And I said: Yea, thou knowest that I believe all the words of my father.

6 And when I had spoken these words, the Spirit cried with a loud voice, saying: Hosanna to the Lord, the most high God; for he is God over all the earth, yea, even above all. And blessed art thou, Nephi, because thou believest in the Son of the most high God; wherefore, thou shalt behold the things which thou hast desired.

7 And behold this thing shall be given unto thee for a sign, that after thou hast beheld the tree which bore the fruit which thy father tasted, thou shalt also behold a man descending out of heaven, and him shall ye witness; and after ye have witnessed him ye shall bear record that it is the Son of God.

8 And it came to pass that the Spirit said unto me: Look! And I looked and beheld a tree; and it was like unto the tree which my father had seen; and the beauty thereof was far beyond, yea, exceeding of all beauty; and the whiteness thereof did exceed the whiteness of the driven snow.

9 And it came to pass after I had seen the tree, I said unto the Spirit: I behold thou hast shown unto me the tree which is precious above all.

10 And he said unto me: What desirest thou?

11 And I said unto him: To know the interpretation thereof—for I spake unto him as a man speaketh; for I beheld that he was in the form of a man; yet nevertheless, I knew that it was the Spirit of the Lord; and he spake unto me as a man speaketh with another.

12 And it came to pass that he said unto me: Look! And I looked as if to look upon him, and I saw him not; for he had gone from before my presence.

13 And it came to pass that I looked and beheld the great city of Jerusalem, and also other cities. And I beheld the city of Nazareth; and in the city of Nazareth I beheld a virgin, and she was exceedingly fair and white.

Date _____
☐ Completed

Date _____
☐ Completed

Date _____
☐ Completed

14 And it came to pass that I saw the heavens open; and an angel came down and stood before me; and he said unto me: Nephi, what beholdest thou?

15 And I said unto him: A virgin, most beautiful and fair above all other virgins.

16 And he said unto me: Knowest thou the condescension of God?

17 And I said unto him: I know that he loveth his children; nevertheless, I do not know the meaning of all things.

18 And he said unto me: Behold, the virgin whom thou seest is the mother of the Son of God, after the manner of the flesh.

19 And it came to pass that I beheld that she was carried away in the Spirit; and after she had been carried away in the Spirit for the space of a time the angel spake unto me, saying: Look!

20 And I looked and beheld the virgin again, bearing a child in her arms.

21 And the angel said unto me: Behold the Lamb of God, yea, even the Son of the Eternal Father! Knowest thou the meaning of the tree which thy father saw?

22 And I answered him, saying: Yea, it is the love of God, which sheddeth itself abroad in the hearts of the children of men; wherefore, it is the most desirable above all things.

23 And he spake unto me, saying: Yea, and the most joyous to the soul.

24 And after he had said these words, he said unto me: Look! And I looked, and I beheld the Son of God going forth among the children of men; and I saw many fall down at his feet and worship him.

25 And it came to pass that I beheld that the rod of iron, which my father had seen, was the word of God, which led to the fountain of living waters, or to the tree of life; which waters are a representation of the love of God; and I also beheld that the tree of life was a representation of the love of God.

26 And the angel said unto me again: Look and behold the condescension of God!

27 And I looked and beheld the Redeemer of the world, of whom my father had spoken; and I also beheld the prophet who should prepare the way before him. And the Lamb of God went forth and was baptized of him; and after he was baptized, I beheld the heavens open, and the Holy Ghost come down out of heaven and abide upon him in the form of a dove.

28 And I beheld that he went forth ministering unto the people, in power and great glory; and the multitudes were gathered together to hear him; and I beheld that they cast him out from among them.

Notes

Date _____
☐ Completed

Date _____
☐ Completed

Date _____
☐ Completed

45

29 And I also beheld twelve others following him. And it came to pass that they were carried away in the Spirit from before my face, and I saw them not.

30 And it came to pass that the angel spake unto me again, saying: Look! And I looked, and I beheld the heavens open again, and I saw angels descending upon the children of men; and they did minister unto them.

31 And he spake unto me again, saying: Look! And I looked, and I beheld the Lamb of God going forth among the children of men. And I beheld multitudes of people who were sick, and who were afflicted with all manner of diseases, and with devils and unclean spirits; and the angel spake and showed all these things unto me. And they were healed by the power of the Lamb of God; and the devils and the unclean spirits were cast out.

32 And it came to pass that the angel spake unto me again, saying: Look! And I looked and beheld the Lamb of God, that he was taken by the people; yea, the Son of the everlasting God was judged of the world; and I saw and bear record.

33 And I, Nephi, saw that he was lifted up upon the cross and slain for the sins of the world.

34 And after he was slain I saw the multitudes of the earth, that they were gathered together to fight against the apostles of the Lamb; for thus were the twelve called by the angel of the Lord.

35 And the multitude of the earth was gathered together; and I beheld that they were in a large and spacious building, like unto the building which my father saw. And the angel of the Lord spake unto me again, saying: Behold the world and the wisdom thereof; yea, behold the house of Israel hath gathered together to fight against the twelve apostles of the Lamb.

36 And it came to pass that I saw and bear record, that the great and spacious building was the pride of the world; and it fell, and the fall thereof was exceedingly great. And the angel of the Lord spake unto me again, saying: Thus shall be the destruction of all nations, kindreds, tongues, and people, that shall fight against the twelve apostles of the Lamb.

Date _____
☐ Completed

Date _____
☐ Completed

Date _____
☐ Completed

1 Nephi

Chapter 12

Sight (Memorization) Words

to

Word Pattern

Pattern	-id
Pattern words in scriptures	**did**
Location in chapter	Verses 3–4, 19
Other words made from this patterns not found in chapter	bid, hid, kid, slid, grid, skid

Phonics Application

- *Short vowel sounds:* the sound of the letter phonetically (versus the long sound or name of the letter).
  - The short sound of I (example: h**i**t)
- *Consonant-Vowel-Consonant:* taking letters, phonetically saying them out loud, and bringing the sounds together to form words.
- *Blend-Vowel-Consonant:* a blend is the combination of two (or more) consonants together. These are the blends: BL, CL, FL, GL, PL, SL, BR, CR, DR, FR, GR, PR, TR, SC, SK, SM, SN, SP, ST, SW, TW.
- *Consonant Diagraphs:* diagraphs are two letters that make one sound. The diagraphs are TH, CH, SH, WH.
- *Complex Consonants:* blends that include three consonants, two consonants that sounds like a single letter, and consonant and vowel clusters. The complex consonants are QU.

Recommended (Age Appropriate) Reading Chunks

- Verses 1–3
- Verses 4–7
- Verses 8–11
- Verses 12–16
- Verses 17–19
- Verses 20–23

Gospel Principle Review/Activity

- What are some of the things that the angel shows Nephi? Do you see these things today?
- *Activity:* Open a newspaper and see if you can see any of the "signs of the times" that Nephi told us about.

Word Patterns

_it

Lesson 12: words made with –it word pattern.
Use alphabet letters to create words.

48

1 Nephi 12

1 And it came to pass that the angel said unto me: Look, and behold thy seed, and also the seed of thy brethren. And I looked and beheld the land of promise; and I beheld multitudes of people, yea, even as it were in number as many as the sand of the sea.

2 And it came to pass that I beheld multitudes gathered together to battle, one against the other; and I beheld wars, and rumors of wars, and great slaughters with the sword among my people.

3 And it came to pass that I beheld many generations pass away, after the manner of wars and contentions in the land; and I beheld many cities, yea, even that I did not number them.

4 And it came to pass that I saw a mist of darkness on the face of the land of promise; and I saw lightnings, and I heard thunderings, and earthquakes, and all manner of tumultuous noises; and I saw the earth and the rocks, that they rent; and I saw mountains tumbling into pieces; and I saw the plains of the earth, that they were broken up; and I saw many cities that they were sunk; and I saw many that they were burned with fire; and I saw many that did tumble to the earth, because of the quaking thereof.

5 And it came to pass after I saw these things, I saw the vapor of darkness, that it passed from off the face of the earth; and behold, I saw multitudes who had not fallen because of the great and terrible judgments of the Lord.

6 And I saw the heavens open, and the Lamb of God descending out of heaven; and he came down and showed himself unto them.

7 And I also saw and bear record that the Holy Ghost fell upon twelve others; and they were ordained of God, and chosen.

8 And the angel spake unto me, saying: Behold the Twelve Disciples of the Lamb, who are chosen to minister unto thy seed.

9 And he said unto me: Thou rememberest the Twelve Apostles of the Lamb? Behold they are they who shall judge the twelve tribes of Israel; wherefore, the twelve ministers of thy seed shall be judged of them; for ye are of the house of Israel.

10 And these twelve ministers whom thou beholdest shall judge thy seed. And, behold, they are righteous forever; for because of their faith in the Lamb of God their garments are made white in his blood.

11 And the angel said unto me: Look! And I looked, and beheld three generations pass away in righteousness; and their garments were white even like unto the Lamb of God. And the angel said unto me: These are made white in the blood of the Lamb, because of their faith in him.

Date _____
☐ Completed

Date _____
☐ Completed

Date _____
☐ Completed

12 And I, Nephi, also saw many of the fourth generation who passed away in righteousness.

13 And it came to pass that I saw the multitudes of the earth gathered together.

14 And the angel said unto me: Behold thy seed, and also the seed of thy brethren.

15 And it came to pass that I looked and beheld the people of my seed gathered together in multitudes against the seed of my brethren; and they were gathered together to battle.

16 And the angel spake unto me, saying: Behold the fountain of filthy water which thy father saw; yea, even the river of which he spake; and the depths thereof are the depths of hell.

17 And the mists of darkness are the temptations of the devil, which blindeth the eyes, and hardeneth the hearts of the children of men, and leadeth them away into broad roads, that they perish and are lost.

18 And the large and spacious building, which thy father saw, is vain imaginations and the pride of the children of men. And a great and a terrible gulf divideth them; yea, even the word of the justice of the Eternal God, and the Messiah who is the Lamb of God, of whom the Holy Ghost beareth record, from the beginning of the world until this time, and from this time henceforth and forever.

19 And while the angel spake these words, I beheld and saw that the seed of my brethren did contend against my seed, according to the word of the angel; and because of the pride of my seed, and the temptations of the devil, I beheld that the seed of my brethren did overpower the people of my seed.

20 And it came to pass that I beheld, and saw the people of the seed of my brethren that they had overcome my seed; and they went forth in multitudes upon the face of the land.

21 And I saw them gathered together in multitudes; and I saw wars and rumors of wars among them; and in wars and rumors of wars I saw many generations pass away.

22 And the angel said unto me: Behold these shall dwindle in unbelief.

23 And it came to pass that I beheld, after they had dwindled in unbelief they became a dark, and loathsome, and a filthy people, full of idleness and all manner of abominations.

Notes

Date _____
☐ Completed

Date _____
☐ Completed

Date _____
☐ Completed

1 Nephi

Chapter 13

Sight (Memorization) Words

from

Word Pattern

Pattern	-it
Pattern words in scriptures	**it**
Location in chapter	Verses 1, 4, 6, 10–16, 20, 23–24, 29, 34, 38–39
Other words made from this patterns not found in chapter	bit, fit, hit, kit, lit, pit, sit, wit, zit, slit, grit, skit, spit

Phonics Application

- *Short vowel sounds:* the sound of the letter phonetically (versus the long sound or name of the letter).
  - The short sound of I (example: hit)
- *Consonant-Vowel-Consonant:* taking letters, phonetically saying them out loud, and bringing the sounds together to form words.
- *Blend-Vowel-Consonant:* a blend is the combination of two (or more) consonants together. These are the blends: BL, CL, FL, GL, PL, SL, BR, CR, DR, FR, GR, PR, TR, SC, SK, SM, SN, SP, ST, SW, TW.
- *Consonant Diagraphs:* diagraphs are two letters that make one sound. The diagraphs are TH, CH, SH, WH.
- *Complex Consonants:* blends that include three consonants, two consonants that sounds like a single letter, and consonant and vowel clusters. The complex consonants are QU.

Recommended (Age Appropriate) Reading Chunks

- Verses 1–5
- Verses 6–10
- Verses 11–14
- Verses 15–19
- Verses 20–23
- Verses 24–26
- Verses 27–29
- Verses 30–32
- Verses 33–35
- Verses 36–39
- Verses 40–42

Gospel Principle Review/Activity

- What is a nation and what is a kingdom? Is there a difference?
- *Activity:* Ask a parent to explain what type of government you live under.

Word Patterns

__it

Lesson 13: words made with –it word pattern.
Use alphabet letters to create words.

1 Nephi 13

1 And it came to pass that the angel spake unto me, saying: Look! And I looked and beheld many nations and kingdoms.

2 And the angel said unto me: What beholdest thou? And I said: I behold many nations and kingdoms.

3 And he said unto me: These are the nations and kingdoms of the Gentiles.

4 And it came to pass that I saw among the nations of the Gentiles the formation of a great church.

5 And the angel said unto me: Behold the formation of a church which is most abominable above all other churches, which slayeth the saints of God, yea, and tortureth them and bindeth them down, and yoketh them with a yoke of iron, and bringeth them down into captivity.

6 And it came to pass that I beheld this great and abominable church; and I saw the devil that he was the founder of it.

7 And I also saw gold, and silver, and silks, and scarlets, and fine-twined linen, and all manner of precious clothing; and I saw many harlots.

8 And the angel spake unto me, saying: Behold the gold, and the silver, and the silks, and the scarlets, and the fine-twined linen, and the precious clothing, and the harlots, are the desires of this great and abominable church.

9 And also for the praise of the world do they destroy the saints of God, and bring them down into captivity.

10 And it came to pass that I looked and beheld many waters; and they divided the Gentiles with the seed of my brethren.

11 And it came to pass that the angel said unto me: Behold the wrath of God is upon the seed of thy brethren.

12 And I looked and beheld a man among the Gentiles, who was separated with the seed of my brethren by the many waters; and I beheld the Spirit of God, that it came down and wrought upon the man; and he went forth upon the many waters, even unto the seed of my brethren, who were in the promised land.

13 And it came to pass that I beheld the Spirit of God, that it wrought upon other Gentiles; and they went forth out of captivity, upon the many waters.

14 And it came to pass that I beheld many multitudes of the Gentiles upon the land of promise; and I beheld the wrath of God, that it was upon the seed of my brethren; and they were scattered before the Gentiles and were smitten.

Date _____
☐ Completed

Date _____
☐ Completed

Date _____
☐ Completed

15 And I beheld the Spirit of the Lord, that it was upon the Gentiles, and they did prosper and obtain the land for their inheritance; and I beheld that they were white, and exceedingly fair and beautiful, like unto my people before they were slain.

16 And it came to pass that I, Nephi, beheld that the Gentiles who had gone forth out of captivity did humble themselves before the Lord; and the power of the Lord was with them.

17 And I beheld that their mother Gentiles were gathered together upon the waters, and upon the land also, to battle against them.

18 And I beheld that the power of God was with them, and also that the wrath of God was upon all those that were gathered together against them to battle.

19 And I, Nephi, beheld that the Gentiles that had gone out of captivity were delivered by the power of God out of the hands of all other nations.

20 And it came to pass that I, Nephi, beheld that they did prosper in the land; and I beheld a book, and it was carried forth among them.

21 And the angel said unto me: Knowest thou the meaning of the book?

22 And I said unto him: I know not.

23 And he said: Behold it proceedeth out of the mouth of a Jew. And I, Nephi, beheld it; and he said unto me: The book that thou beholdest is a record of the Jews, which contains the covenants of the Lord, which he hath made unto the house of Israel; and it also containeth many of the prophecies of the holy prophets; and it is a record like unto the engravings which are upon the plates of brass, save there are not so many; nevertheless, they contain the covenants of the Lord, which he hath made unto the house of Israel; wherefore, they are of great worth unto the Gentiles.

24 And the angel of the Lord said unto me: Thou hast beheld that the book proceeded forth with the mouth of a Jew; and when it proceeded forth with the mouth of a Jew it contained the fulness of the gospel of the Lord, of whom the twelve apostles bear record; and they bear record according to the truth which is in the Lamb of God.

25 Wherefore, these things go forth with the Jews in purity unto the Gentiles, according to the truth which is in God.

26 And after they go forth by the hand of the twelve apostles of the Lamb, with the Jews unto the Gentiles, thou seest the formation of that great and abominable church, which is most abominable above all other churches; for behold, they have taken away with the gospel of the Lamb many parts which are plain and most precious; and also many covenants of the Lord have they taken away.

Notes

Date _____
☐ Completed

Date _____
☐ Completed

Date _____
☐ Completed

27 And all this have they done that they might pervert the right ways of the Lord, that they might blind the eyes and harden the hearts of the children of men.

28 Wherefore, thou seest that after the book hath gone forth through the hands of the great and abominable church, that there are many plain and precious things taken away with the book, which is the book of the Lamb of God.

29 And after these plain and precious things were taken away it goeth forth unto all the nations of the Gentiles; and after it goeth forth unto all the nations of the Gentiles, yea, even across the many waters which thou hast seen with the Gentiles which have gone forth out of captivity, thou seest—because of the many plain and precious things which have been taken out of the book, which were plain unto the understanding of the children of men, according to the plainness which is in the Lamb of God—because of these things which are taken away out of the gospel of the Lamb, an exceedingly great many do stumble, yea, insomuch that Satan hath great power over them.

30 Nevertheless, thou beholdest that the Gentiles who have gone forth out of captivity, and have been lifted up by the power of God above all other nations, upon the face of the land which is choice above all other lands, which is the land that the Lord God hath covenanted with thy father that his seed should have for the land of their inheritance; wherefore, thou seest that the Lord God will not suffer that the Gentiles will utterly destroy the mixture of thy seed, which are among thy brethren.

31 Neither will he suffer that the Gentiles shall destroy the seed of thy brethren.

32 Neither will the Lord God suffer that the Gentiles shall forever remain in that awful state of blindness, which thou beholdest they are in, because of the plain and most precious parts of the gospel of the Lamb which have been kept back by that abominable church, whose formation thou hast seen.

33 Wherefore saith the Lamb of God: I will be merciful unto the Gentiles, unto the visiting of the remnant of the house of Israel in great judgment.

34 And it came to pass that the angel of the Lord spake unto me, saying: Behold, saith the Lamb of God, after I have visited the remnant of the house of Israel—and this remnant of whom I speak is the seed of thy father—wherefore, after I have visited them in judgment, and smitten them by the hand of the Gentiles, and after the Gentiles do stumble exceedingly, because of the most plain and precious parts of the gospel of the Lamb which have been kept back by that abominable church, which is the mother of harlots, saith the Lamb—I will be merciful unto the Gentiles in that day, insomuch that I will bring forth unto them, in mine

Date _____
☐ Completed

Date _____
☐ Completed

own power, much of my gospel, which shall be plain and precious, saith the Lamb.

35 For, behold, saith the Lamb: I will manifest myself unto thy seed, that they shall write many things which I shall minister unto them, which shall be plain and precious; and after thy seed shall be destroyed, and dwindle in unbelief, and also the seed of thy brethren, behold, these things shall be hid up, to come forth unto the Gentiles, by the gift and power of the Lamb.

36 And in them shall be written my gospel, saith the Lamb, and my rock and my salvation.

37 And blessed are they who shall seek to bring forth my Zion at that day, for they shall have the gift and the power of the Holy Ghost; and if they endure unto the end they shall be lifted up at the last day, and shall be saved in the everlasting kingdom of the Lamb; and whoso shall publish peace, yea, tidings of great joy, how beautiful upon the mountains shall they be.

38 And it came to pass that I beheld the remnant of the seed of my brethren, and also the book of the Lamb of God, which had proceeded forth with the mouth of the Jew, that it came forth with the Gentiles unto the remnant of the seed of my brethren.

39 And after it had come forth unto them I beheld other books, which came forth by the power of the Lamb, with the Gentiles unto them, unto the convincing of the Gentiles and the remnant of the seed of my brethren, and also the Jews who were scattered upon all the face of the earth, that the records of the prophets and of the twelve apostles of the Lamb are true.

40 And the angel spake unto me, saying: These last records, which thou hast seen among the Gentiles, shall establish the truth of the first, which are of the twelve apostles of the Lamb, and shall make known the plain and precious things which have been taken away with them; and shall make known to all kindreds, tongues, and people, that the Lamb of God is the Son of the Eternal Father, and the Savior of the world; and that all men must come unto him, or they cannot be saved.

41 And they must come according to the words which shall be established by the mouth of the Lamb; and the words of the Lamb shall be made known in the records of thy seed, as well as in the records of the twelve apostles of the Lamb; wherefore they both shall be established in one; for there is one God and one Shepherd over all the earth.

42 And the time cometh that he shall manifest himself unto all nations, both unto the Jews and also unto the Gentiles; and after he has manifested himself unto the Jews and also unto the Gentiles, then he shall manifest himself unto the Gentiles and also unto the Jews, and the last shall be first, and the first shall be last.

Date _____
☐ Completed

Date _____
☐ Completed

Date _____
☐ Completed

1 Nephi

Chapter 14

Sight (Memorization) Words

wo

(Note: see phonics application for a pattern for this sight word.)

Word Pattern

Pattern	-if
Pattern words in scriptures	**if**
Location in chapter	Verse 37
Other words made from this patterns not found in chapter	(none listed)

Phonics Application

- *Words that end with vowels:* when a word ends with a vowel and it is the only vowel in the word, the vowel is usually a LONG vowel, or a vowel that says its name (example: wo).
- *Short vowel sounds:* the sound of the letter phonetically (versus the long sound or name of the letter).
  - The short sound of I (example: h**i**t).
- *Consonant-Vowel-Consonant:* taking letters, phonetically saying them out loud, and bringing the sounds together to form words.
- *Blend-Vowel-Consonant:* a blend is the combination of two (or more) consonants together. These are the blends: BL, CL, FL, GL, PL, SL, BR, CR, DR, FR, GR, PR, TR, SC, SK, SM, SN, SP, ST, SW, TW.
- *Consonant* Diagraphs: diagraphs are two letters that make one sound. The diagraphs are TH, CH, SH, WH.
- *Complex Consonants:* blends that include three consonants, two consonants that sounds like a single letter, and consonant and vowel clusters. The complex consonants are QU.

Recommended (Age Appropriate) Reading Chunks

- Verses 1–3
- Verses 4–7
- Verses 8–11
- Verses 12–14
- Verses 15–17
- Verses 18–22
- Verses 23–26
- Verses 27–30

Gospel Principle Review/Activity

- What does the angel tell Nephi?
- *Activity:* Make a visual depiction of the Twelve Tribes. Use cutouts or drawings to help you illustrate what the Twelve Tribes or the House of Israel is. (Refer to Genesis 35 for names.)

Word Patterns

if

Lesson 14: words made with –if word pattern.
Use alphabet letters to create words.

1 Nephi 14

1 And it shall come to pass, that if the Gentiles shall hearken unto the Lamb of God in that day that he shall manifest himself unto them in word, and also in power, in very deed, unto the taking away of their stumbling blocks—

2 And harden not their hearts against the Lamb of God, they shall be numbered among the seed of thy father; yea, they shall be numbered among the house of Israel; and they shall be a blessed people upon the promised land forever; they shall be no more brought down into captivity; and the house of Israel shall no more be confounded.

3 And that great pit, which hath been digged for them by that great and abominable church, which was founded by the devil and his children, that he might lead away the souls of men down to hell—yea, that great pit which hath been digged for the destruction of men shall be filled by those who digged it, unto their utter destruction, saith the Lamb of God; not the destruction of the soul, save it be the casting of it into that hell which hath no end.

4 For behold, this is according to the captivity of the devil, and also according to the justice of God, upon all those who will work wickedness and abomination before him.

5 And it came to pass that the angel spake unto me, Nephi, saying: Thou hast beheld that if the Gentiles repent it shall be well with them; and thou also knowest concerning the covenants of the Lord unto the house of Israel; and thou also hast heard that whoso repenteth not must perish.

6 Therefore, wo be unto the Gentiles if it so be that they harden their hearts against the Lamb of God.

7 For the time cometh, saith the Lamb of God, that I will work a great and a marvelous work among the children of men; a work which shall be everlasting, either on the one hand or on the other—either to the convincing of them unto peace and life eternal, or unto the deliverance of them to the hardness of their hearts and the blindness of their minds unto their being brought down into captivity, and also into destruction, both temporally and spiritually, according to the captivity of the devil, of which I have spoken.

8 And it came to pass that when the angel had spoken these words, he said unto me: Rememberest thou the covenants of the Father unto the house of Israel? I said unto him, Yea.

9 And it came to pass that he said unto me: Look, and behold that great and abominable church, which is the mother of abominations, whose founder is the devil.

Date _____
☐ Completed

Date _____
☐ Completed

10 And he said unto me: Behold there are save two churches only; the one is the church of the Lamb of God, and the other is the church of the devil; wherefore, whoso belongeth not to the church of the Lamb of God belongeth to that great church, which is the mother of abominations; and she is the whore of all the earth.

11 And it came to pass that I looked and beheld the whore of all the earth, and she sat upon many waters; and she had dominion over all the earth, among all nations, kindreds, tongues, and people.

12 And it came to pass that I beheld the church of the Lamb of God, and its numbers were few, because of the wickedness and abominations of the whore who sat upon many waters; nevertheless, I beheld that the church of the Lamb, who were the saints of God, were also upon all the face of the earth; and their dominions upon the face of the earth were small, because of the wickedness of the great whore whom I saw.

13 And it came to pass that I beheld that the great mother of abominations did gather together multitudes upon the face of all the earth, among all the nations of the Gentiles, to fight against the Lamb of God.

14 And it came to pass that I, Nephi, beheld the power of the Lamb of God, that it descended upon the saints of the church of the Lamb, and upon the covenant people of the Lord, who were scattered upon all the face of the earth; and they were armed with righteousness and with the power of God in great glory.

15 And it came to pass that I beheld that the wrath of God was poured out upon that great and abominable church, insomuch that there were wars and rumors of wars among all the nations and kindreds of the earth.

16 And as there began to be wars and rumors of wars among all the nations which belonged to the mother of abominations, the angel spake unto me, saying: Behold, the wrath of God is upon the mother of harlots; and behold, thou seest all these things—

17 And when the day cometh that the wrath of God is poured out upon the mother of harlots, which is the great and abominable church of all the earth, whose founder is the devil, then, at that day, the work of the Father shall commence, in preparing the way for the fulfilling of his covenants, which he hath made to his people who are of the house of Israel.

18 And it came to pass that the angel spake unto me, saying: Look!

19 And I looked and beheld a man, and he was dressed in a white robe.

20 And the angel said unto me: Behold one of the twelve apostles of the Lamb.

Date _____
☐ Completed

Date _____
☐ Completed

Date _____
☐ Completed

21 Behold, he shall see and write the remainder of these things; yea, and also many things which have been.

22 And he shall also write concerning the end of the world.

_____

23 Wherefore, the things which he shall write are just and true; and behold they are written in the book which thou beheld proceeding out of the mouth of the Jew; and at the time they proceeded out of the mouth of the Jew, or, at the time the book proceeded out of the mouth of the Jew, the things which were written were plain and pure, and most precious and easy to the understanding of all men.

24 And behold, the things which this apostle of the Lamb shall write are many things which thou hast seen; and behold, the remainder shalt thou see.

25 But the things which thou shalt see hereafter thou shalt not write; for the Lord God hath ordained the apostle of the Lamb of God that he should write them.

26 And also others who have been, to them hath he shown all things, and they have written them; and they are sealed up to come forth in their purity, according to the truth which is in the Lamb, in the own due time of the Lord, unto the house of Israel.

_____

27 And I, Nephi, heard and bear record, that the name of the apostle of the Lamb was John, according to the word of the angel.

28 And behold, I, Nephi, am forbidden that I should write the remainder of the things which I saw and heard; wherefore the things which I have written sufficeth me; and I have written but a small part of the things which I saw.

29 And I bear record that I saw the things which my father saw, and the angel of the Lord did make them known unto me.

30 And now I make an end of speaking concerning the things which I saw while I was carried away in the spirit; and if all the things which I saw are not written, the things which I have written are true. And thus it is. Amen.

Date _____
☐ Completed

Date _____
☐ Completed

1 Nephi

Chapter 15

Sight (Memorization) Words

Word Pattern

Pattern	-od
Pattern words in scriptures	**God**
Location in chapter	Verses 15, 24–25, 28, 30, 33–36
Other words made from this patterns not found in chapter	nod, pod, rod, sod

Phonics Application

- *Short vowel sounds:* the sound of the letter phonetically (versus the long sound or name of the letter).
  - The short sound of O (example: h**o**p)
- *Consonant-Vowel-Consonant:* taking letters, phonetically saying them out loud, and bringing the sounds together to form words.
- *Blend-Vowel-Consonant*: a blend is the combination of two (or more) consonants together. These are the blends: BL, CL, FL, GL, PL, SL, BR, CR, DR, FR, GR, PR, TR, SC, SK, SM, SN, SP, ST, SW, TW.
- *Consonant Diagraphs*: diagraphs are two letters that make one sound. The diagraphs are TH, CH, SH, WH.
- *Complex Consonants*: blends that include three consonants, two consonants that sounds like a single letter, and consonant and vowel clusters. The complex consonants are QU.

Recommended (Age Appropriate) Reading Chunks

- Verses 1–5
- Verses 6–11
- Verses 12–14
- Verses 15–18
- Verses 19–23
- Verses 24–28
- Verses 29–32
- Verses 33–36

Gospel Principle Review/Activity

- Who are the Jews? How do they relate to the House of Israel?
- *Activity:* Which House do you belong to? Fill in the blank and make a cut out of your "House."

HOUSE OF _____ (last name)

Word Patterns

_od

Lesson 15: words made with –od word pattern.
Use alphabet letters to create words.

1 Nephi 15

1 And it came to pass that after I, Nephi, had been carried away in the spirit, and seen all these things, I returned to the tent of my father.

2 And it came to pass that I beheld my brethren, and they were disputing one with another concerning the things which my father had spoken unto them.

3 For he truly spake many great things unto them, which were hard to be understood, save a man should inquire of the Lord; and they being hard in their hearts, therefore they did not look unto the Lord as they ought.

4 And now I, Nephi, was grieved because of the hardness of their hearts, and also, because of the things which I had seen, and knew they must unavoidably come to pass because of the great wickedness of the children of men.

5 And it came to pass that I was overcome because of my afflictions, for I considered that mine afflictions were great above all, because of the destruction of my people, for I had beheld their fall.

6 And it came to pass that after I had received strength I spake unto my brethren, desiring to know of them the cause of their disputations.

7 And they said: Behold, we cannot understand the words which our father hath spoken concerning the natural branches of the olive-tree, and also concerning the Gentiles.

8 And I said unto them: Have ye inquired of the Lord?

9 And they said unto me: We have not; for the Lord maketh no such thing known unto us.

10 Behold, I said unto them: How is it that ye do not keep the commandments of the Lord? How is it that ye will perish, because of the hardness of your hearts?

11 Do ye not remember the things which the Lord hath said?—If ye will not harden your hearts, and ask me in faith, believing that ye shall receive, with diligence in keeping my commandments, surely these things shall be made known unto you.

12 Behold, I say unto you, that the house of Israel was compared unto an olive-tree, by the Spirit of the Lord which was in our father; and behold are we not broken off from the house of Israel, and are we not a branch of the house of Israel?

13 And now, the thing which our father meaneth concerning the grafting in of the natural branches through the fulness of the Gentiles, is, that in the latter days, when our seed shall have dwindled in unbelief, yea, for the space of many years, and many generations after the Messiah shall be manifested in body unto the children of men, then shall the fulness of the gospel of the Messiah come unto the Gentiles, and from the Gentiles unto the remnant of our seed—

Notes

Date _____
☐ Completed

Date _____
☐ Completed

14 And at that day shall the remnant of our seed know that they are of the house of Israel, and that they are the covenant people of the Lord; and then shall they know and come to the knowledge of their forefathers, and also to the knowledge of the gospel of their Redeemer, which was ministered unto their fathers by him; wherefore, they shall come to the knowledge of their Redeemer and the very points of his doctrine, that they may know how to come unto him and be saved.

15 And then at that day will they not rejoice and give praise unto their everlasting God, their rock and their salvation? Yea, at that day, will they not receive the strength and nourishment from the true vine? Yea, will they not come unto the true fold of God?

16 Behold, I say unto you, Yea; they shall be remembered again among the house of Israel; they shall be grafted in, being a natural branch of the olive-tree, into the true olive-tree.

17 And this is what our father meaneth; and he meaneth that it will not come to pass until after they are scattered by the Gentiles; and he meaneth that it shall come by way of the Gentiles, that the Lord may show his power unto the Gentiles, for the very cause that he shall be rejected of the Jews, or of the house of Israel.

18 Wherefore, our father hath not spoken of our seed alone, but also of all the house of Israel, pointing to the covenant which should be fulfilled in the latter days; which covenant the Lord made to our father Abraham, saying: In thy seed shall all the kindreds of the earth be blessed.

19 And it came to pass that I, Nephi, spake much unto them concerning these things; yea, I spake unto them concerning the restoration of the Jews in the latter days.

20 And I did rehearse unto them the words of Isaiah, who spake concerning the restoration of the Jews, or of the house of Israel; and after they were restored they should no more be confounded, neither should they be scattered again. And it came to pass that I did speak many words unto my brethren, that they were pacified and did humble themselves before the Lord.

21 And it came to pass that they did speak unto me again, saying: What meaneth this thing which our father saw in a dream? What meaneth the tree which he saw?

22 And I said unto them: It was a representation of the tree of life.

23 And they said unto me: What meaneth the rod of iron which our father saw, that led to the tree?

24 And I said unto them that it was the word of God; and whoso would hearken unto the word of God, and would hold fast unto it, they would never perish; neither could the temptations and the fiery darts of the adver-

Notes

Date _____
☐ Completed

Date _____
☐ Completed

Date _____
☐ Completed

sary overpower them unto blindness, to lead them away to destruction.

25 Wherefore, I, Nephi, did exhort them to give heed unto the word of the Lord; yea, I did exhort them with all the energies of my soul, and with all the faculty which I possessed, that they would give heed to the word of God and remember to keep his commandments always in all things.

26 And they said unto me: What meaneth the river of water which our father saw?

27 And I said unto them that the water which my father saw was filthiness; and so much was his mind swallowed up in other things that he beheld not the filthiness of the water.

28 And I said unto them that it was an awful gulf, which separated the wicked from the tree of life, and also from the saints of God.

Date _____
☐ Completed

29 And I said unto them that it was a representation of that awful hell, which the angel said unto me was prepared for the wicked.

30 And I said unto them that our father also saw that the justice of God did also divide the wicked from the righteous; and the brightness thereof was like unto the brightness of a flaming fire, which ascendeth up unto God forever and ever, and hath no end.

31 And they said unto me: Doth this thing mean the torment of the body in the days of probation, or doth it mean the final state of the soul after the death of the temporal body, or doth it speak of the things which are temporal?

32 And it came to pass that I said unto them that it was a representation of things both temporal and spiritual; for the day should come that they must be judged of their works, yea, even the works which were done by the temporal body in their days of probation.

Date _____
☐ Completed

33 Wherefore, if they should die in their wickedness they must be cast off also, as to the things which are spiritual, which are pertaining to righteousness; wherefore, they must be brought to stand before God, to be judged of their works; and if their works have been filthiness they must needs be filthy; and if they be filthy it must needs be that they cannot dwell in the kingdom of God; if so, the kingdom of God must be filthy also.

34 But behold, I say unto you, the kingdom of God is not filthy, and there cannot any unclean thing enter into the kingdom of God; wherefore there must needs be a place of filthiness prepared for that which is filthy.

35 And there is a place prepared, yea, even that awful hell of which I have spoken, and the devil is the preparator of it; wherefore the final state of the souls of men is to dwell in the kingdom of God, or to be cast out because of that justice of which I have spoken.

36 Wherefore, the wicked are rejected from the righteous, and also from that tree of life, whose fruit is most precious and most desirable above all other fruits; yea, and it is the greatest of all the gifts of God. And thus I spake unto my brethren. Amen.

Notes

Date _____
☐ Completed

1 Nephi

Chapter 16

Sight (Memorization) Words

want	walk

Word Pattern

Pattern	-op
Pattern words in scriptures	**top**
Location in chapter	Verse 30
Other words made from this patterns not found in chapter	cop, hop, mop, pop, flop, plop, slop, crop, drop, prop, stop, chop, shop

Phonics Application

- *Short vowel sounds:* the sound of the letter phonetically (versus the long sound or name of the letter).
  - The short sound of O (example: h**o**p)
- *Consonant-Vowel-Consonant:* taking letters, phonetically saying them out loud, and bringing the sounds together to form words.
- *Blend-Vowel-Consonant:* a blend is the combination of two (or more) consonants together. These are the blends: BL, CL, FL, GL, PL, SL, BR, CR, DR, FR, GR, PR, TR, SC, SK, SM, SN, SP, ST, SW, TW.
- *Consonant Diagraphs:* diagraphs are two letters that make one sound. The diagraphs are TH, CH, SH, WH.
- *Complex Consonants:* blends that include three consonants, two consonants that sounds like a single letter, and consonant and vowel clusters. The complex consonants are QU.

Recommended (Age Appropriate) Reading Chunks

- Verses 1–4
- Verses 5–9
- Verses 10–13
- Verses 14–17
- Verses 18–21
- Verses 22–25
- Verses 26–29
- Verses 30–34
- Verses 35–37
- Verses 38–39

Gospel Principle Review/Activity

- Why is marriage important? Why would the Lord make Nephi and his brothers go back to Jerusalem to get Ishmael and his family?
- *Activity:* Ask someone who is married to show you his or her wedding album and to share how important this day was to him or her.

Word Patterns

of

Lesson 16: words made with –of word pattern.
Use alphabet letters to create words.

1 Nephi 16

1 And now it came to pass that after I, Nephi, had made an end of speaking to my brethren, behold they said unto me: Thou hast declared unto us hard things, more than we are able to bear.

2 And it came to pass that I said unto them that I knew that I had spoken hard things against the wicked, according to the truth; and the righteous have I justified, and testified that they should be lifted up at the last day; wherefore, the guilty taketh the truth to be hard, for it cutteth them to the very center.

3 And now my brethren, if ye were righteous and were willing to hearken to the truth, and give heed unto it, that ye might walk uprightly before God, then ye would not murmur because of the truth, and say: Thou speakest hard things against us.

4 And it came to pass that I, Nephi, did exhort my brethren, with all diligence, to keep the commandments of the Lord.

5 And it came to pass that they did humble themselves before the Lord; insomuch that I had joy and great hopes of them, that they would walk in the paths of righteousness.

6 Now, all these things were said and done as my father dwelt in a tent in the valley which he called Lemuel.

7 And it came to pass that I, Nephi, took one of the daughters of Ishmael to wife; and also, my brethren took of the daughters of Ishmael to wife; and also Zoram took the eldest daughter of Ishmael to wife.

8 And thus my father had fulfilled all the commandments of the Lord which had been given unto him. And also, I, Nephi, had been blessed of the Lord exceedingly.

9 And it came to pass that the voice of the Lord spake unto my father by night, and commanded him that on the morrow he should take his journey into the wilderness.

10 And it came to pass that as my father arose in the morning, and went forth to the tent door, to his great astonishment he beheld upon the ground a round ball of curious workmanship; and it was of fine brass. And within the ball were two spindles; and the one pointed the way whither we should go into the wilderness.

11 And it came to pass that we did gather together whatsoever things we should carry into the wilderness, and all the remainder of our provisions which the Lord had given unto us; and we did take seed of every kind that we might carry into the wilderness.

12 And it came to pass that we did take our tents and depart into the wilderness, across the river Laman.

Date _____
☐ Completed

Date _____
☐ Completed

13 And it came to pass that we traveled for the space of four days, nearly a south–southeast direction, and we did pitch our tents again; and we did call the name of the place Shazer.

14 And it came to pass that we did take our bows and our arrows, and go forth into the wilderness to slay food for our families; and after we had slain food for our families we did return again to our families in the wilderness, to the place of Shazer. And we did go forth again in the wilderness, following the same direction, keeping in the most fertile parts of the wilderness, which were in the borders near the Red Sea.

15 And it came to pass that we did travel for the space of many days, slaying food by the way, with our bows and our arrows and our stones and our slings.

16 And we did follow the directions of the ball, which led us in the more fertile parts of the wilderness.

17 And after we had traveled for the space of many days, we did pitch our tents for the space of a time, that we might again rest ourselves and obtain food for our families.

18 And it came to pass that as I, Nephi, went forth to slay food, behold, I did break my bow, which was made of fine steel; and after I did break my bow, behold, my brethren were angry with me because of the loss of my bow, for we did obtain no food.

19 And it came to pass that we did return without food to our families, and being much fatigued, because of their journeying, they did suffer much for the want of food.

20 And it came to pass that Laman and Lemuel and the sons of Ishmael did begin to murmur exceedingly, because of their sufferings and afflictions in the wilderness; and also my father began to murmur against the Lord his God; yea, and they were all exceedingly sorrowful, even that they did murmur against the Lord.

21 Now it came to pass that I, Nephi, having been afflicted with my brethren because of the loss of my bow, and their bows having lost their springs, it began to be exceedingly difficult, yea, insomuch that we could obtain no food.

22 And it came to pass that I, Nephi, did speak much unto my brethren, because they had hardened their hearts again, even unto complaining against the Lord their God.

23 And it came to pass that I, Nephi, did make out of wood a bow, and out of a straight stick, an arrow; wherefore, I did arm myself with a bow and an arrow, with a sling and with stones. And I said unto my father: Whither shall I go to obtain food?

Notes

Date _____
☐ Completed
_____
_____
_____
_____
_____
_____
_____
_____
_____
_____

Date _____
☐ Completed
_____
_____
_____
_____
_____
_____
_____
_____
_____
_____

Date _____
☐ Completed
_____
_____
_____
_____
_____
_____
_____

24 And it came to pass that he did inquire of the Lord, for they had humbled themselves because of my words; for I did say many things unto them in the energy of my soul.

25 And it came to pass that the voice of the Lord came unto my father; and he was truly chastened because of his murmuring against the Lord, insomuch that he was brought down into the depths of sorrow.

26 And it came to pass that the voice of the Lord said unto him: Look upon the ball, and behold the things which are written.

27 And it came to pass that when my father beheld the things which were written upon the ball, he did fear and tremble exceedingly, and also my brethren and the sons of Ishmael and our wives.

28 And it came to pass that I, Nephi, beheld the pointers which were in the ball, that they did work according to the faith and diligence and heed which we did give unto them.

29 And there was also written upon them a new writing, which was plain to be read, which did give us understanding concerning the ways of the Lord; and it was written and changed from time to time, according to the faith and diligence which we gave unto it. And thus we see that by small means the Lord can bring about great things.

30 And it came to pass that I, Nephi, did go forth up into the top of the mountain, according to the directions which were given upon the ball.

31 And it came to pass that I did slay wild beasts, insomuch that I did obtain food for our families.

32 And it came to pass that I did return to our tents, bearing the beasts which I had slain; and now when they beheld that I had obtained food, how great was their joy! And it came to pass that they did humble themselves before the Lord, and did give thanks unto him.

33 And it came to pass that we did again take our journey, traveling nearly the same course as in the beginning; and after we had traveled for the space of many days we did pitch our tents again, that we might tarry for the space of a time.

34 And it came to pass that Ishmael died, and was buried in the place which was called Nahom.

35 And it came to pass that the daughters of Ishmael did mourn exceedingly, because of the loss of their father, and because of their afflictions in the wilderness; and they did murmur against my father, because he had brought them out of the land of Jerusalem, saying: Our father is dead; yea, and we have wandered much in the wilderness, and we have suffered much affliction, hunger, thirst, and fatigue; and after all these sufferings we must perish in the wilderness with hunger.

Notes

Date _____
☐ Completed

Date _____
☐ Completed

Date _____
☐ Completed

36 And thus they did murmur against my father, and also against me; and they were desirous to return again to Jerusalem.

37 And Laman said unto Lemuel and also unto the sons of Ishmael: Behold, let us slay our father, and also our brother Nephi, who has taken it upon him to be our ruler and our teacher, who are his elder brethren.

---

38 Now, he says that the Lord has talked with him, and also that angels have ministered unto him. But behold, we know that he lies unto us; and he tells us these things, and he worketh many things by his cunning arts, that he may deceive our eyes, thinking, perhaps, that he may lead us away into some strange wilderness; and after he has led us away, he has thought to make himself a king and a ruler over us, that he may do with us according to his will and pleasure. And after this manner did my brother Laman stir up their hearts to anger.

39 And it came to pass that the Lord was with us, yea, even the voice of the Lord came and did speak many words unto them, and did chasten them exceedingly; and after they were chastened by the voice of the Lord they did turn away their anger, and did repent of their sins, insomuch that the Lord did bless us again with food, that we did not perish.

Date _____
☐ Completed

Date _____
☐ Completed

1 Nephi

Chapter 17

Sight (Memorization) Words

be

(Note: see phonics application for a pattern for this sight word.)

Word Pattern

Pattern	-ot
Pattern words in scriptures	**not**
Location in chapter	Verses 5, 12, 18–19, 23–24, 31, 43, 45, 48, 52–55
Other words made from this patterns not found in chapter	cot, dot, got, hot, jot, lot, pot, rot, tot, blot, clot, plot, slot, trot, snot, spot, shot

Phonics Application

- *Words that end with vowels:* when a word ends with a vowel and it is the only vowel in the word, the vowel is usually a LONG vowel, or a vowel that says its name (example: b**e**).
- *Short vowel sounds:* the sound of the letter phonetically (versus the long sound or name of the letter).
  - The short sound of O (example: h**o**p)
- *Consonant-Vowel-Consonant:* taking letters, phonetically saying them out loud, and bringing the sounds together to form words.
- *Blend-Vowel-Consonant:* a blend is the combination of two (or more) consonants together. These are the blends: BL, CL, FL, GL, PL, SL, BR, CR, DR, FR, GR, PR, TR, SC, SK, SM, SN, SP, ST, SW, TW.
- *Consonant Diagraphs:* diagraphs are two letters that make one sound. The diagraphs are TH, CH, SH, WH.
- *Complex Consonants:* blends that include three consonants, two consonants that sounds like a single letter, and consonant and vowel clusters. The complex consonants are QU.

Recommended (Age Appropriate) Reading Chunks

- Verses 1–3
- Verses 4–7
- Verses 8–10
- Verses 11–14
- Verses 15–18
- Verses 19–20
- Verses 21–23
- Verses 24–28
- Verses 29–31
- Verses 32–35
- Verses 36–40
- Verses 41–43
- Verses 44–46
- Verses 47–49
- Verses 50–52
- Verses 53–55

Gospel Principle Review/Activity

- How did Nephi know how to build a ship? How do the Lord and the Holy Ghost direct us?
- *Activity:* Get some Popsicle sticks and glue. Without any plans, see if you can build a ship just like Nephi did.

Word Patterns

_ot

Lesson 17: words made with –ot word pattern.
Use alphabet letters to create words.

1 Nephi 17

1 And it came to pass that we did again take our journey in the wilderness; and we did travel nearly eastward from that time forth. And we did travel and wade through much affliction in the wilderness; and our women did bear children in the wilderness.

2 And so great were the blessings of the Lord upon us, that while we did live upon raw meat in the wilderness, our women did give plenty of suck for their children, and were strong, yea, even like unto the men; and they began to bear their journeyings without murmurings.

3 And thus we see that the commandments of God must be fulfilled. And if it so be that the children of men keep the commandments of God he doth nourish them, and strengthen them, and provide means whereby they can accomplish the thing which he has commanded them; wherefore, he did provide means for us while we did sojourn in the wilderness.

4 And we did sojourn for the space of many years, yea, even eight years in the wilderness.

5 And we did come to the land which we called Bountiful, because of its much fruit and also wild honey; and all these things were prepared of the Lord that we might not perish. And we beheld the sea, which we called Irreantum, which, being interpreted, is many waters.

6 And it came to pass that we did pitch our tents by the seashore; and notwithstanding we had suffered many afflictions and much difficulty, yea, even so much that we cannot write them all, we were exceedingly rejoiced when we came to the seashore; and we called the place Bountiful, because of its much fruit.

7 And it came to pass that after I, Nephi, had been in the land of Bountiful for the space of many days, the voice of the Lord came unto me, saying: Arise, and get thee into the mountain. And it came to pass that I arose and went up into the mountain, and cried unto the Lord.

8 And it came to pass that the Lord spake unto me, saying: Thou shalt construct a ship, after the manner which I shall show thee, that I may carry thy people across these waters.

9 And I said: Lord, whither shall I go that I may find ore to molten, that I may make tools to construct the ship after the manner which thou hast shown unto me?

10 And it came to pass that the Lord told me whither I should go to find ore, that I might make tools.

11 And it came to pass that I, Nephi, did make a bellows wherewith to blow the fire, of the skins of beasts; and after I had made a bellows, that

Date _____
☐ Completed

Date _____
☐ Completed

Date _____
☐ Completed

I might have wherewith to blow the fire, I did smite two stones together that I might make fire.

12 For the Lord had not hitherto suffered that we should make much fire, as we journeyed in the wilderness; for he said: I will make thy food become sweet, that ye cook it not;

13 And I will also be your light in the wilderness; and I will prepare the way before you, if it so be that ye shall keep my commandments; wherefore, inasmuch as ye shall keep my commandments ye shall be led towards the promised land; and ye shall know that it is by me that ye are led.

14 Yea, and the Lord said also that: After ye have arrived in the promised land, ye shall know that I, the Lord, am God; and that I, the Lord, did deliver you from destruction; yea, that I did bring you out of the land of Jerusalem.

---

15 Wherefore, I, Nephi, did strive to keep the commandments of the Lord, and I did exhort my brethren to faithfulness and diligence.

16 And it came to pass that I did make tools of the ore which I did molten out of the rock.

17 And when my brethren saw that I was about to build a ship, they began to murmur against me, saying: Our brother is a fool, for he thinketh that he can build a ship; yea, and he also thinketh that he can cross these great waters.

18 And thus my brethren did complain against me, and were desirous that they might not labor, for they did not believe that I could build a ship; neither would they believe that I was instructed of the Lord.

---

19 And now it came to pass that I, Nephi, was exceedingly sorrowful because of the hardness of their hearts; and now when they saw that I began to be sorrowful they were glad in their hearts, insomuch that they did rejoice over me, saying: We knew that ye could not construct a ship, for we knew that ye were lacking in judgment; wherefore, thou canst not accomplish so great a work.

20 And thou art like unto our father, led away by the foolish imaginations of his heart; yea, he hath led us out of the land of Jerusalem, and we have wandered in the wilderness for these many years; and our women have toiled, being big with child; and they have borne children in the wilderness and suffered all things, save it were death; and it would have been better that they had died before they came out of Jerusalem than to have suffered these afflictions.

---

21 Behold, these many years we have suffered in the wilderness, which time we might have enjoyed our possessions and the land of our inheritance; yea, and we might have been happy.

Notes

Date _____
☐ Completed

Date _____
☐ Completed

Date _____
☐ Completed

22 And we know that the people who were in the land of Jerusalem were a righteous people; for they kept the statutes and judgments of the Lord, and all his commandments, according to the law of Moses; wherefore, we know that they are a righteous people; and our father hath judged them, and hath led us away because we would hearken unto his words; yea, and our brother is like unto him. And after this manner of language did my brethren murmur and complain against us.

23 And it came to pass that I, Nephi, spake unto them, saying: Do ye believe that our fathers, who were the children of Israel, would have been led away out of the hands of the Egyptians if they had not hearkened unto the words of the Lord?

24 Yea, do ye suppose that they would have been led out of bondage, if the Lord had not commanded Moses that he should lead them out of bondage?

25 Now ye know that the children of Israel were in bondage; and ye know that they were laden with tasks, which were grievous to be borne; wherefore, ye know that it must needs be a good thing for them, that they should be brought out of bondage.

26 Now ye know that Moses was commanded of the Lord to do that great work; and ye know that by his word the waters of the Red Sea were divided hither and thither, and they passed through on dry ground.

27 But ye know that the Egyptians were drowned in the Red Sea, who were the armies of Pharaoh.

28 And ye also know that they were fed with manna in the wilderness.

29 Yea, and ye also know that Moses, by his word according to the power of God which was in him, smote the rock, and there came forth water, that the children of Israel might quench their thirst.

30 And notwithstanding they being led, the Lord their God, their Redeemer, going before them, leading them by day and giving light unto them by night, and doing all things for them which were expedient for man to receive, they hardened their hearts and blinded their minds, and reviled against Moses and against the true and living God.

31 And it came to pass that according to his word he did destroy them; and according to his word he did lead them; and according to his word he did do all things for them; and there was not any thing done save it were by his word.

32 And after they had crossed the river Jordan he did make them mighty unto the driving out of the children of the land, yea, unto the scattering them to destruction.

33 And now, do ye suppose that the children of this land, who were in

Notes

_____
_____
_____
_____
_____
_____
_____

Date _____
☐ Completed

_____
_____
_____
_____
_____
_____
_____
_____

Date _____
☐ Completed

_____
_____
_____
_____
_____
_____
_____

Date _____
☐ Completed

_____
_____
_____

the land of promise, who were driven out by our fathers, do ye suppose that they were righteous? Behold, I say unto you, Nay.

34 Do ye suppose that our fathers would have been more choice than they if they had been righteous? I say unto you, Nay.

35 Behold, the Lord esteemeth all flesh in one; he that is righteous is favored of God. But behold, this people had rejected every word of God, and they were ripe in iniquity; and the fulness of the wrath of God was upon them; and the Lord did curse the land against them, and bless it unto our fathers; yea, he did curse it against them unto their destruction, and he did bless it unto our fathers unto their obtaining power over it.

36 Behold, the Lord hath created the earth that it should be inhabited; and he hath created his children that they should possess it.

37 And he raiseth up a righteous nation, and destroyeth the nations of the wicked.

38 And he leadeth away the righteous into precious lands, and the wicked he destroyeth, and curseth the land unto them for their sakes.

39 He ruleth high in the heavens, for it is his throne, and this earth is his footstool.

40 And he loveth those who will have him to be their God. Behold, he loved our fathers, and he covenanted with them, yea, even Abraham, Isaac, and Jacob; and he remembered the covenants which he had made; wherefore, he did bring them out of the land of Egypt.

41 And he did straiten them in the wilderness with his rod; for they hardened their hearts, even as ye have; and the Lord straitened them because of their iniquity. He sent fiery flying serpents among them; and after they were bitten he prepared a way that they might be healed; and the labor which they had to perform was to look; and because of the simpleness of the way, or the easiness of it, there were many who perished.

42 And they did harden their hearts from time to time, and they did revile against Moses, and also against God; nevertheless, ye know that they were led forth by his matchless power into the land of promise.

43 And now, after all these things, the time has come that they have become wicked, yea, nearly unto ripeness; and I know not but they are at this day about to be destroyed; for I know that the day must surely come that they must be destroyed, save a few only, who shall be led away into captivity.

44 Wherefore, the Lord commanded my father that he should depart into the wilderness; and the Jews also sought to take away his life; yea, and ye also have sought to take away his life; wherefore, ye are murderers in your hearts and ye are like unto them.

Notes

Date _____
☐ Completed

Date _____
☐ Completed

Date _____
☐ Completed

45 Ye are swift to do iniquity but slow to remember the Lord your God. Ye have seen an angel, and he spake unto you; yea, ye have heard his voice from time to time; and he hath spoken unto you in a still small voice, but ye were past feeling, that ye could not feel his words; wherefore, he has spoken unto you like unto the voice of thunder, which did cause the earth to shake as if it were to divide asunder.

46 And ye also know that by the power of his almighty word he can cause the earth that it shall pass away; yea, and ye know that by his word he can cause the rough places to be made smooth, and smooth places shall be broken up. O, then, why is it, that ye can be so hard in your hearts?

47 Behold, my soul is rent with anguish because of you, and my heart is pained; I fear lest ye shall be cast off forever. Behold, I am full of the Spirit of God, insomuch that my frame has no strength.

48 And now it came to pass that when I had spoken these words they were angry with me, and were desirous to throw me into the depths of the sea; and as they came forth to lay their hands upon me I spake unto them, saying: In the name of the Almighty God, I command you that ye touch me not, for I am filled with the power of God, even unto the consuming of my flesh; and whoso shall lay his hands upon me shall wither even as a dried reed; and he shall be as naught before the power of God, for God shall smite him.

49 And it came to pass that I, Nephi, said unto them that they should murmur no more against their father; neither should they withhold their labor from me, for God had commanded me that I should build a ship.

50 And I said unto them: If God had commanded me to do all things I could do them. If he should command me that I should say unto this water, be thou earth, it should be earth; and if I should say it, it would be done.

51 And now, if the Lord has such great power, and has wrought so many miracles among the children of men, how is it that he cannot instruct me, that I should build a ship?

52 And it came to pass that I, Nephi, said many things unto my brethren, insomuch that they were confounded and could not contend against me; neither durst they lay their hands upon me nor touch me with their fingers, even for the space of many days. Now they durst not do this lest they should wither before me, so powerful was the Spirit of God; and thus it had wrought upon them.

53 And it came to pass that the Lord said unto me: Stretch forth thine hand again unto thy brethren, and they shall not wither before thee, but I will shock them, saith the Lord, and this will I do, that they may know that I am the Lord their God.

Date _____
☐ Completed

Date _____
☐ Completed

Date _____
☐ Completed

54 And it came to pass that I stretched forth my hand unto my brethren, and they did not wither before me; but the Lord did shake them, even according to the word which he had spoken.

55 And now, they said: We know of a surety that the Lord is with thee, for we know that it is the power of the Lord that has shaken us. And they fell down before me, and were about to worship me, but I would not suffer them, saying: I am thy brother, yea, even thy younger brother; wherefore, worship the Lord thy God, and honor thy father and thy mother, that thy days may be long in the land which the Lord thy God shall give thee.

Date _____
☐ Completed

1 Nephi

Chapter 18

Sight (Memorization) Words

Word Pattern

Pattern	-on
Pattern words in scriptures	**on**
Location in chapter	Verse 26
Exceptions to the rule	gone
Other words made from this patterns not found in chapter	Don, Ron

Phonics Application

- *Words that end with vowels:* when a word ends with a vowel and it is the only vowel in the word, the vowel usually is a LONG vowel, or a vowel that says its name (example: b**y**).
- *Short vowel sounds:* the sound of the letter phonetically (versus the long sound or name of the letter).
  - The short sound of O (example: h**o**p)
- *Consonant-Vowel-Consonant:* taking letters, phonetically saying them out loud, and bringing the sounds together to form words.
- *Blend-Vowel-Consonant:* a blend is the combination of two (or more) consonants together. These are the blends: BL, CL, FL, GL, PL, SL, BR, CR, DR, FR, GR, PR, TR, SC, SK, SM, SN, SP, ST, SW, TW.
- *Consonant Diagraphs:* diagraphs are two letters that make one sound. The diagraphs are TH, CH, SH, WH.
- *Complex Consonants:* blends that include three consonants, two consonants that sounds like a single letter, and consonant and vowel clusters. The complex consonants are QU.

Recommended (Age Appropriate) Reading Chunks

- Verses 1–4
- Verses 5–8
- Verses 9–12
- Verses 13–15
- Verses 16–19
- Verses 20–23
- Verses 24–25

Gospel Principle Review/Activity

- What would you have done if you saw your brother Nephi being tied up?
- *Activity:* If you were taking a large trip (like Nephi and his family did), what things would you need to pack? Make a list of the items you imagine that Nephi and his family had to take. Make a second list of the things you would need to bring on a trip. Are the items on these two lists different?

Word Patterns

__on

Lesson 18: words made with –on word pattern.
Use alphabet letters to create words.

1 Nephi 18

1 And it came to pass that they did worship the Lord, and did go forth with me; and we did work timbers of curious workmanship. And the Lord did show me from time to time after what manner I should work the timbers of the ship.

2 Now I, Nephi, did not work the timbers after the manner which was learned by men, neither did I build the ship after the manner of men; but I did build it after the manner which the Lord had shown unto me; wherefore, it was not after the manner of men.

3 And I, Nephi, did go into the mount oft, and I did pray oft unto the Lord; wherefore the Lord showed unto me great things.

4 And it came to pass that after I had finished the ship, according to the word of the Lord, my brethren beheld that it was good, and that the workmanship thereof was exceedingly fine; wherefore, they did humble themselves again before the Lord.

5 And it came to pass that the voice of the Lord came unto my father, that we should arise and go down into the ship.

6 And it came to pass that on the morrow, after we had prepared all things, much fruits and meat from the wilderness, and honey in abundance, and provisions according to that which the Lord had commanded us, we did go down into the ship, with all our loading and our seeds, and whatsoever thing we had brought with us, every one according to his age; wherefore, we did all go down into the ship, with our wives and our children.

7 And now, my father had begat two sons in the wilderness; the elder was called Jacob and the younger Joseph.

8 And it came to pass after we had all gone down into the ship, and had taken with us our provisions and things which had been commanded us, we did put forth into the sea and were driven forth before the wind towards the promised land.

9 And after we had been driven forth before the wind for the space of many days, behold, my brethren and the sons of Ishmael and also their wives began to make themselves merry, insomuch that they began to dance, and to sing, and to speak with much rudeness, yea, even that they did forget by what power they had been brought thither; yea, they were lifted up unto exceeding rudeness.

10 And I, Nephi, began to fear exceedingly lest the Lord should be angry with us, and smite us because of our iniquity, that we should be swallowed up in the depths of the sea; wherefore, I, Nephi, began to speak to them with much soberness; but behold they were angry with me, saying: We will not that our younger brother shall be a ruler over us.

Date _____
☐ Completed

Date _____
☐ Completed

11 And it came to pass that Laman and Lemuel did take me and bind me with cords, and they did treat me with much harshness; nevertheless, the Lord did suffer it that he might show forth his power, unto the fulfilling of his word which he had spoken concerning the wicked.

12 And it came to pass that after they had bound me insomuch that I could not move, the compass, which had been prepared of the Lord, did cease to work.

---

13 Wherefore, they knew not whither they should steer the ship, insomuch that there arose a great storm, yea, a great and terrible tempest, and we were driven back upon the waters for the space of three days; and they began to be frightened exceedingly lest they should be drowned in the sea; nevertheless they did not loose me.

14 And on the fourth day, which we had been driven back, the tempest began to be exceedingly sore.

15 And it came to pass that we were about to be swallowed up in the depths of the sea. And after we had been driven back upon the waters for the space of four days, my brethren began to see that the judgments of God were upon them, and that they must perish save that they should repent of their iniquities; wherefore, they came unto me, and loosed the bands which were upon my wrists, and behold they had swollen exceedingly; and also mine ankles were much swollen, and great was the soreness thereof.

---

17 Now my father, Lehi, had said many things unto them, and also unto the sons of Ishmael; but, behold, they did breathe out much threatenings against anyone that should speak for me; and my parents being stricken in years, and having suffered much grief because of their children, they were brought down, yea, even upon their sick–beds.

18 Because of their grief and much sorrow, and the iniquity of my brethren, they were brought near even to be carried out of this time to meet their God; yea, their grey hairs were about to be brought down to lie low in the dust; yea, even they were near to be cast with sorrow into a watery grave.

19 And Jacob and Joseph also, being young, having need of much nourishment, were grieved because of the afflictions of their mother; and also my wife with her tears and prayers, and also my children, did not soften the hearts of my brethren that they would loose me.

---

20 And there was nothing save it were the power of God, which threatened them with destruction, could soften their hearts; wherefore, when they saw that they were about to be swallowed up in the depths of the sea they repented of the thing which they had done, insomuch that they loosed me.

Notes

Date _____
☐ Completed

Date _____
☐ Completed

Date _____
☐ Completed

21   And it came to pass after they had loosed me, behold, I took the compass, and it did work whither I desired it. And it came to pass that I prayed unto the Lord; and after I had prayed the winds did cease, and the storm did cease, and there was a great calm.

22   And it came to pass that I, Nephi, did guide the ship, that we sailed again towards the promised land.

23   And it came to pass that after we had sailed for the space of many days we did arrive at the promised land; and we went forth upon the land, and did pitch our tents; and we did call it the promised land.

24   And it came to pass that we did begin to till the earth, and we began to plant seeds; yea, we did put all our seeds into the earth, which we had brought from the land of Jerusalem. And it came to pass that they did grow exceedingly; wherefore, we were blessed in abundance.

25   And it came to pass that we did find upon the land of promise, as we journeyed in the wilderness, that there were beasts in the forests of every kind, both the cow and the ox, and the ass and the horse, and the goat and the wild goat, and all manner of wild animals, which were for the use of men. And we did find all manner of ore, both of gold, and of silver, and of copper.

Date _____
☐ Completed

Date _____
☐ Completed

1 Nephi

Chapter 19

Sight (Memorization) Words

are

(Note: the AR pattern is related to the R-controlled vowels explained in Mosiah 12.)

Word Pattern

Pattern	-ut
Pattern words in scriptures	**but**
Location in chapter	Verses 6–7, 23
Exceptions to the rule	put
Other words made from this patterns not found in chapter	cut, glut, gut, hut, nut, rut, shut

Phonics Application

- *Short vowel sounds:* the sound of the letter phonetically (versus the long sound or name of the letter).
  - The short sound of U (example: c**u**p)
- *Consonant-Vowel-Consonant:* taking letters, phonetically saying them out loud, and bringing the sounds together to form words.
- *Blend-Vowel-Consonant:* a blend is the combination of two (or more) consonants together. These are the blends: BL, CL, FL, GL, PL, SL, BR, CR, DR, FR, GR, PR, TR, SC, SK, SM, SN, SP, ST, SW, TW.
- *Consonant Diagraphs:* diagraphs are two letters that make one sound. The diagraphs are TH, CH, SH, WH.
- *Complex Consonants:* blends that include three consonants, two consonants that sounds like a single letter, and consonant and vowel clusters. The complex consonants are QU.

Recommended (Age Appropriate) Reading Chunks

- Verses 1–3
- Verses 4–6
- Verses 7–10
- Verses 11–14
- Verses 15-20
- Verses 21–24

Gospel Principle Review/Activity

- When did the prophets say that the God of Israel would come? Did He come then?
- What will happen to the Jews in the last days?
- *Activity:* Choose one or two important things that the latter-day prophets have said and record these teachings in your journal like Nephi did.

Word Patterns

ut

Lesson 19: words made with –ut word pattern.
Use alphabet letters to create words.

1 Nephi 19

1 And it came to pass that the Lord commanded me, wherefore I did make plates of ore that I might engraven upon them the record of my people. And upon the plates which I made I did engraven the record of my father, and also our journeyings in the wilderness, and the prophecies of my father; and also many of mine own prophecies have I engraven upon them.

2 And I knew not at the time when I made them that I should be commanded of the Lord to make these plates; wherefore, the record of my father, and the genealogy of his fathers, and the more part of all our proceedings in the wilderness are engraven upon those first plates of which I have spoken; wherefore, the things which transpired before I made these plates are, of a truth, more particularly made mention upon the first plates.

3 And after I had made these plates by way of commandment, I, Nephi, received a commandment that the ministry and the prophecies, the more plain and precious parts of them, should be written upon these plates; and that the things which were written should be kept for the instruction of my people, who should possess the land, and also for other wise purposes, which purposes are known unto the Lord.

4 Wherefore, I, Nephi, did make a record upon the other plates, which gives an account, or which gives a greater account of the wars and contentions and destructions of my people. And this have I done, and commanded my people what they should do after I was gone; and that these plates should be handed down from one generation to another, or from one prophet to another, until further commandments of the Lord.

5 And an account of my making these plates shall be given hereafter; and then, behold, I proceed according to that which I have spoken; and this I do that the more sacred things may be kept for the knowledge of my people.

6 Nevertheless, I do not write anything upon plates save it be that I think it be sacred. And now, if I do err, even did they err of old; not that I would excuse myself because of other men, but because of the weakness which is in me, according to the flesh, I would excuse myself.

7 For the things which some men esteem to be of great worth, both to the body and soul, others set at naught and trample under their feet. Yea, even the very God of Israel do men trample under their feet; I say, trample under their feet but I would speak in other words—they set him at naught, and hearken not to the voice of his counsels.

8 And behold he cometh, according to the words of the angel, in six

Date _____
☐ Completed

Date _____
☐ Completed

hundred years from the time my father left Jerusalem.

9 And the world, because of their iniquity, shall judge him to be a thing of naught; wherefore they scourge him, and he suffereth it; and they smite him, and he suffereth it. Yea, they spit upon him, and he suffereth it, because of his loving kindness and his long-suffering towards the children of men.

10 And the God of our fathers, who were led out of Egypt, out of bondage, and also were preserved in the wilderness by him, yea, the God of Abraham, and of Isaac, and the God of Jacob, yieldeth himself, according to the words of the angel, as a man, into the hands of wicked men, to be lifted up, according to the words of Zenock, and to be crucified, according to the words of Neum, and to be buried in a sepulchre, according to the words of Zenos, which he spake concerning the three days of darkness, which should be a sign given of his death unto those who should inhabit the isles of the sea, more especially given unto those who are of the house of Israel.

11 For thus spake the prophet: The Lord God surely shall visit all the house of Israel at that day, some with his voice, because of their righteousness, unto their great joy and salvation, and others with the thunderings and the lightnings of his power, by tempest, by fire, and by smoke, and vapor of darkness, and by the opening of the earth, and by mountains which shall be carried up.

12 And all these things must surely come, saith the prophet Zenos. And the rocks of the earth must rend; and because of the groanings of the earth, many of the kings of the isles of the sea shall be wrought upon by the Spirit of God, to exclaim: The God of nature suffers.

13 And as for those who are at Jerusalem, saith the prophet, they shall be scourged by all people, because they crucify the God of Israel, and turn their hearts aside, rejecting signs and wonders, and the power and glory of the God of Israel.

14 And because they turn their hearts aside, saith the prophet, and have despised the Holy One of Israel, they shall wander in the flesh, and perish, and become a hiss and a byword, and be hated among all nations.

15 Nevertheless, when that day cometh, saith the prophet, that they no more turn aside their hearts against the Holy One of Israel, then will he remember the covenants which he made to their fathers.

16 Yea, then will he remember the isles of the sea; yea, and all the people who are of the house of Israel, will I gather in, saith the Lord, according to the words of the prophet Zenos, from the four quarters of the earth.

17 Yea, and all the earth shall see the salvation of the Lord, saith the prophet; every nation, kindred, tongue and people shall be blessed.

18 And I, Nephi, have written these things unto my people, that perhaps

89

Date _____
☐ Completed

Date _____
☐ Completed

I might persuade them that they would remember the Lord their Redeemer.

19 Wherefore, I speak unto all the house of Israel, if it so be that they should obtain these things.

20 For behold, I have workings in the spirit, which doth weary me even that all my joints are weak, for those who are at Jerusalem; for had not the Lord been merciful, to show unto me concerning them, even as he had prophets of old, I should have perished also.

_____

21 And he surely did show unto the prophets of old all things concerning them; and also he did show unto many concerning us; wherefore, it must needs be that we know concerning them for they are written upon the plates of brass.

22 Now it came to pass that I, Nephi, did teach my brethren these things; and it came to pass that I did read many things to them, which were engraven upon the plates of brass, that they might know concerning the doings of the Lord in other lands, among people of old.

23 And I did read many things unto them which were written in the books of Moses; but that I might more fully persuade them to believe in the Lord their Redeemer I did read unto them that which was written by the prophet Isaiah; for I did liken all scriptures unto us, that it might be for our profit and learning.

24 Wherefore I spake unto them, saying: Hear ye the words of the prophet, ye who are a remnant of the house of Israel, a branch who have been broken off; hear ye the words of the prophet, which were written unto all the house of Israel, and liken them unto yourselves, that ye may have hope as well as your brethren from whom ye have been broken off; for after this manner has the prophet written.

Date _____
☐ Completed

Date _____
☐ Completed

1 Nephi

Chapter 20

Sight (Memorization) Words

all

(Also: ball, call, fall, gall, hall, tall, wall, small—see rule in the Phonics Application.)

Word Pattern

Pattern	-up
Pattern words in scriptures	**up**
Location in chapter	Verse 13
Other words made from this patterns not found in chapter	cup, pup

Phonics Application

- *Rule:* in words that end in ALL, the A makes the short O sound.
- *Short vowel sounds:* the sound of the letter phonetically (versus the long sound or name of the letter).
  - The short sound of U (example: c**u**p)
- *Consonant-Vowel-Consonant:* taking letters, phonetically saying them out loud, and bringing the sounds together to form words.
- *Blend-Vowel-Consonant:* a blend is the combination of two (or more) consonants together. These are the blends: BL, CL, FL, GL, PL, SL, BR, CR, DR, FR, GR, PR, TR, SC, SK, SM, SN, SP, ST, SW, TW.
- *Consonant Diagraphs:* diagraphs are two letters that make one sound. The diagraphs are TH, CH, SH, WH.
- *Complex Consonants:* blends that include three consonants, two consonants that sounds like a single letter, and consonant and vowel clusters. The complex consonants are QU.

Recommended (Age Appropriate) Reading Chunks

- Verses 1–5
- Verses 6–10
- Verses 11–16
- Verses 17–22

Gospel Principle Review/Activity

- Who is Isaiah and why is Nephi quoting him? (Refer to Bible Dictionary under "Isaiah.")
- What does Isaiah teach us?
- *Activity:* Do our prophets today quote other prophets of old? Read the following quote to see who President Hinckley is quoting: "The Savior taught of leaving the ninety and nine to find the lost sheep, that forgiveness and restitution might come. Isaiah declared, . . . 'Come now, and let us reason together, saith the Lord: though your sins be as scarlet, they shall be as white as snow; though they be red like crimson, they shall be as wool' (Isaiah 1:16–18)"[3]

Word Patterns

__ up

Lesson 20: words made with –up word pattern.
Use alphabet letters to create words.

1 Nephi 20

1 Hearken and hear this, O house of Jacob, who are called by the name of Israel, and are come forth out of the waters of Judah, or out of the waters of baptism, who swear by the name of the Lord, and make mention of the God of Israel, yet they swear not in truth nor in righteousness.

2 Nevertheless, they call themselves of the holy city, but they do not stay themselves upon the God of Israel, who is the Lord of Hosts; yea, the Lord of Hosts is his name.

3 Behold, I have declared the former things from the beginning; and they went forth out of my mouth, and I showed them. I did show them suddenly.

4 And I did it because I knew that thou art obstinate, and thy neck is an iron sinew, and thy brow brass;

5 And I have even from the beginning declared to thee; before it came to pass I showed them thee; and I showed them for fear lest thou shouldst say—Mine idol hath done them, and my graven image, and my molten image hath commanded them.

6 Thou hast seen and heard all this; and will ye not declare them? And that I have showed thee new things from this time, even hidden things, and thou didst not know them.

7 They are created now, and not from the beginning, even before the day when thou heardest them not they were declared unto thee, lest thou shouldst say—Behold I knew them.

8 Yea, and thou heardest not; yea, thou knewest not; yea, from that time thine ear was not opened; for I knew that thou wouldst deal very treacherously, and wast called a transgressor from the womb.

9 Nevertheless, for my name's sake will I defer mine anger, and for my praise will I refrain from thee, that I cut thee not off.

10 For, behold, I have refined thee, I have chosen thee in the furnace of affliction.

11 For mine own sake, yea, for mine own sake will I do this, for I will not suffer my name to be polluted, and I will not give my glory unto another.

12 Hearken unto me, O Jacob, and Israel my called, for I am he; I am the first, and I am also the last.

13 Mine hand hath also laid the foundation of the earth, and my right hand hath spanned the heavens. I call unto them and they stand up together.

14 All ye, assemble yourselves, and hear; who among them hath declared these things unto them? The Lord hath loved him; yea, and he will fulfill

Date _____
☐ Completed

Date _____
☐ Completed

his word which he hath declared by them; and he will do his pleasure on Babylon, and his arm shall come upon the Chaldeans.

15 Also, saith the Lord; I the Lord, yea, I have spoken; yea, I have called him to declare, I have brought him, and he shall make his way prosperous.

16 Come ye near unto me; I have not spoken in secret; from the beginning, from the time that it was declared have I spoken; and the Lord God, and his Spirit, hath sent me.

17 And thus saith the Lord, thy Redeemer, the Holy One of Israel; I have sent him, the Lord thy God who teacheth thee to profit, who leadeth thee by the way thou shouldst go, hath done it.

18 O that thou hadst hearkened to my commandments—then had thy peace been as a river, and thy righteousness as the waves of the sea.

19 Thy seed also had been as the sand; the offspring of thy bowels like the gravel thereof; his name should not have been cut off nor destroyed from before me.

20 Go ye forth of Babylon, flee ye from the Chaldeans, with a voice of singing declare ye, tell this, utter to the end of the earth; say ye: The Lord hath redeemed his servant Jacob.

21 And they thirsted not; he led them through the deserts; he caused the waters to flow out of the rock for them; he clave the rock also and the waters gushed out.

22 And notwithstanding he hath done all this, and greater also, there is no peace, saith the Lord, unto the wicked.

Date _____

☐ Completed

Date _____

☐ Completed

1 Nephi

Chapter 21

Sight (Memorization) Words

her

(Note: the -er pattern is related to the R-controlled vowels explained in Mosiah 11.)

Word Pattern

Pattern	-un
Pattern words in scriptures	**sun**
Location in chapter	Verse 10
Other words made from this patterns not found in chapter	bun, fun, run, sun, spun

Phonics Application

- *Short vowel sounds:* the sound of the letter phonetically (versus the long sound or name of the letter).
  - The short sound of U (example: c**u**p)
- *Consonant-Vowel-Consonant:* taking letters, phonetically saying them out loud, and bringing the sounds together to form words.
- *Blend-Vowel-Consonant:* a blend is the combination of two (or more) consonants together. These are the blends: BL, CL, FL, GL, PL, SL, BR, CR, DR, FR, GR, PR, TR, SC, SK, SM, SN, SP, ST, SW, TW.
- *Consonant Diagraphs:* diagraphs are two letters that make one sound. The diagraphs are TH, CH, SH, WH.
- *Complex Consonants:* blends that include three consonants, two consonants that sounds like a single letter, and consonant and vowel clusters. The complex consonants are QU.

Recommended (Age Appropriate) Reading Chunks

- Verses 1–5
- Verses 6–10
- Verses 11–16
- Verses 17–21
- Verses 22–26

Gospel Principle Review/Activity

- The Messiah is compared to a light in the darkness. What does it mean to compare?
- *Activity:* Think of other things you can compare (or that have something in common). Go on a scavenger hunt and take a sheet of paper with two columns. Find items that you can compare. When you find items that you can compare, write one in each column, list characteristics underneath, then write a paragraph on why you think they are similar.

Word Patterns

un

Lesson 21: words made with –un word pattern.
Use alphabet letters to create words.

1 Nephi 21

1 And again: Hearken, O ye house of Israel, all ye that are broken off and are driven out because of the wickedness of the pastors of my people; yea, all ye that are broken off, that are scattered abroad, who are of my people, O house of Israel. Listen, O isles, unto me, and hearken ye people from far; the Lord hath called me from the womb; from the bowels of my mother hath he made mention of my name.

2 And he hath made my mouth like a sharp sword; in the shadow of his hand hath he hid me, and made me a polished shaft; in his quiver hath he hid me;

3 And said unto me: Thou art my servant, O Israel, in whom I will be glorified.

4 Then I said, I have labored in vain, I have spent my strength for naught and in vain; surely my judgment is with the Lord, and my work with my God.

5 And now, saith the Lord—that formed me from the womb that I should be his servant, to bring Jacob again to him—though Israel be not gathered, yet shall I be glorious in the eyes of the Lord, and my God shall be my strength.

Date _____
☐ Completed

6 And he said: It is a light thing that thou shouldst be my servant to raise up the tribes of Jacob, and to restore the preserved of Israel. I will also give thee for a light to the Gentiles, that thou mayest be my salvation unto the ends of the earth.

7 Thus saith the Lord, the Redeemer of Israel, his Holy One, to him whom man despiseth, to him whom the nations abhorreth, to servant of rulers: Kings shall see and arise, princes also shall worship, because of the Lord that is faithful.

8 Thus saith the Lord: In an acceptable time have I heard thee, O isles of the sea, and in a day of salvation have I helped thee; and I will preserve thee, and give thee my servant for a covenant of the people, to establish the earth, to cause to inherit the desolate heritages;

9 That thou mayest say to the prisoners: Go forth; to them that sit in darkness: Show yourselves. They shall feed in the ways, and their pastures shall be in all high places.

10 They shall not hunger nor thirst, neither shall the heat nor the sun smite them; for he that hath mercy on them shall lead them, even by the springs of water shall he guide them.

Date _____
☐ Completed

11 And I will make all my mountains a way, and my highways shall be exalted.

12 And then, O house of Israel, behold, these shall come from far; and lo, these from the north and from the west; and these from the land of Sinim.

13 Sing, O heavens; and be joyful, O earth; for the feet of those who are

in the east shall be established; and break forth into singing, O mountains; for they shall be smitten no more; for the Lord hath comforted his people, and will have mercy upon his afflicted.

14 But, behold, Zion hath said: The Lord hath forsaken me, and my Lord hath forgotten me—but he will show that he hath not.

15 For can a woman forget her sucking child, that she should not have compassion on the son of her womb? Yea, they may forget, yet will I not forget thee, O house of Israel.

16 Behold, I have graven thee upon the palms of my hands; thy walls are continually before me.

---

17 Thy children shall make haste against thy destroyers; and they that made thee waste shall go forth of thee.

18 Lift up thine eyes round about and behold; all these gather themselves together, and they shall come to thee. And as I live, saith the Lord, thou shalt surely clothe thee with them all, as with an ornament, and bind them on even as a bride.

19 For thy waste and thy desolate places, and the land of thy destruction, shall even now be too narrow by reason of the inhabitants; and they that swallowed thee up shall be far away.

20 The children whom thou shalt have, after thou hast lost the first, shall again in thine ears say: The place is too strait for me; give place to me that I may dwell.

21 Then shalt thou say in thine heart: Who hath begotten me these, seeing I have lost my children, and am desolate, a captive, and removing to and fro? And who hath brought up these? Behold, I was left alone; these, where have they been?

---

22 Thus saith the Lord God: Behold, I will lift up mine hand to the Gentiles, and set up my standard to the people; and they shall bring thy sons in their arms, and thy daughters shall be carried upon their shoulders.

23 And kings shall be thy nursing fathers, and their queens thy nursing mothers; they shall bow down to thee with their face towards the earth, and lick up the dust of thy feet; and thou shalt know that I am the Lord; for they shall not be ashamed that wait for me.

24 For shall the prey be taken from the mighty, or the lawful captives delivered?

25 But thus saith the Lord, even the captives of the mighty shall be taken away, and the prey of the terrible shall be delivered; for I will contend with him that contendeth with thee, and I will save thy children.

26 And I will feed them that oppress thee with their own flesh; they shall be drunken with their own blood as with sweet wine; and all flesh shall know that I, the Lord, am thy Savior and thy Redeemer, the Mighty One of Jacob.

Date _____
☐ Completed

Date _____
☐ Completed

1 Nephi

Chapter 22

Sight (Memorization) Words

my	is	he	his	to	from
wo	you	want	be	by	are
all	her				

Word Pattern—all CVC (Consonant-Vowel-Consonant) and BVC (Blend-Vowel-Consonant) Patterns

A Patterns: -ab, -ad, -ag, -am, -an, -ap, -ar, -at
E Patterns: -ed, -eg, -em, -en, -et
I Patterns: -id, -if, -ig, -im, -in, -ip, -is, -it
O Patterns: -ob, -od, -og, -on, -op, -ot
U Patterns: -ub, -ug, -um, -un, -up, -us, -ut

Phonics Application

- *Short vowel sounds:* the sound of the letter phonetically (versus the long sound or name of the letter).
  - The short sound of A (example: **a**pple)
  - The short sound of E (example: b**e**d)
  - The short sound of I (example: h**i**t)
  - The short sound of O (example: h**o**p)
  - The short sound of U (example: c**u**p)
- *Consonant-Vowel-Consonant:* taking letters, phonetically saying them out loud, and bringing the sounds together to form words.
- *Blend-Vowel-Consonant:* a blend is the combination of two (or more) consonants together. These are the blends: BL, CL, FL, GL, PL, SL, BR, CR, DR, FR, GR, PR, TR, SC, SK, SM, SN, SP, ST, SW, TW.
- *Consonant Diagraphs:* diagraphs are two letters that make one sound. The diagraphs are TH, CH, SH, WH.
- *Complex Consonants:* blends that include three consonants, two consonants that sounds like a single letter, and consonant and vowel clusters. The complex consonants are QU.

Recommended (Age Appropriate) Reading Chunks

- Verses 1–4
- Verses 5–7
- Verses 8–12
- Verses 13–15
- Verses 16–19
- Verses 20–22
- Verses 23–25
- Verses 26–31

Gospel Principle Review/Activity

- What will happen to Israel in the latter days?
- *Activity:* What do you think the world will be like when Satan is bound and there is no more evil? Draw a picture of what the world would look like with no evil.

Word Patterns—Review

Lesson 22 Review: Find the words in the word box in the word search.

Word Box

cup	his	not
Ron	rim	pit
did	mop	sun
God		put

```
O  U  I  D  V  P  X  G  S
I  D  M  I  R  F  O  H  I
U  N  I  R  G  P  I  M  Y
E  U  P  D  O  S  U  W  S
G  U  T  L  D  X  D  T  C
C  V  O  S  U  N  T  Q  F
N  R  T  O  R  W  T  V  W
R  I  L  P  F  U  O  X  E
P  Y  P  R  O  N  N  T  B
```

100

1 Nephi 22

1 And now it came to pass that after I, Nephi, had read these things which were engraven upon the plates of brass, my brethren came unto me and said unto me: What meaneth these things which ye have read? Behold, are they to be understood according to things which are spiritual, which shall come to pass according to the spirit and not the flesh?

2 And I, Nephi, said unto them: Behold they were manifest unto the prophet by the voice of the Spirit; for by the Spirit are all things made known unto the prophets, which shall come upon the children of men according to the flesh.

3 Wherefore, the things of which I have read are things pertaining to things both temporal and spiritual; for it appears that the house of Israel, sooner or later, will be scattered upon all the face of the earth, and also among all nations.

4 And behold, there are many who are already lost from the knowledge of those who are at Jerusalem. Yea, the more part of all the tribes have been led away; and they are scattered to and fro upon the isles of the sea; and whither they are none of us knoweth, save that we know that they have been led away.

5 And since they have been led away, these things have been prophesied concerning them, and also concerning all those who shall hereafter be scattered and be confounded, because of the Holy One of Israel; for against him will they harden their hearts; wherefore, they shall be scattered among all nations and shall be hated of all men.

6 Nevertheless, after they shall be nursed by the Gentiles, and the Lord has lifted up his hand upon the Gentiles and set them up for a standard, and their children have been carried in their arms, and their daughters have been carried upon their shoulders, behold these things of which are spoken are temporal; for thus are the covenants of the Lord with our fathers; and it meaneth us in the days to come, and also all our brethren who are of the house of Israel.

7 And it meaneth that the time cometh that after all the house of Israel have been scattered and confounded, that the Lord God will raise up a mighty nation among the Gentiles, yea, even upon the face of this land; and by them shall our seed be scattered.

8 And after our seed is scattered the Lord God will proceed to do a marvelous work among the Gentiles, which shall be of great worth unto our seed; wherefore, it is likened unto their being nourished by the Gentiles and being carried in their arms and upon their shoulders.

9 And it shall also be of worth unto the Gentiles; and not only unto the

Gentiles but unto all the house of Israel, unto the making known of the covenants of the Father of heaven unto Abraham, saying: In thy seed shall all the kindreds of the earth be blessed.

10 And I would, my brethren, that ye should know that all the kindreds of the earth cannot be blessed unless he shall make bare his arm in the eyes of the nations.

11 Wherefore, the Lord God will proceed to make bare his arm in the eyes of all the nations, in bringing about his covenants and his gospel unto those who are of the house of Israel.

12 Wherefore, he will bring them again out of captivity, and they shall be gathered together to the lands of their inheritance; and they shall be brought out of obscurity and out of darkness; and they shall know that the Lord is their Savior and their Redeemer, the Mighty One of Israel.

13 And the blood of that great and abominable church, which is the whore of all the earth, shall turn upon their own heads; for they shall war among themselves, and the sword of their own hands shall fall upon their own heads, and they shall be drunken with their own blood.

14 And every nation which shall war against thee, O house of Israel, shall be turned one against another, and they shall fall into the pit which they digged to ensnare the people of the Lord. And all that fight against Zion shall be destroyed, and that great whore, who hath perverted the right ways of the Lord, yea, that great and abominable church, shall tumble to the dust and great shall be the fall of it.

15 For behold, saith the prophet, the time cometh speedily that Satan shall have no more power over the hearts of the children of men; for the day soon cometh that all the proud and they who do wickedly shall be as stubble; and the day cometh that they must be burned.

16 For the time soon cometh that the fulness of the wrath of God shall be poured out upon all the children of men; for he will not suffer that the wicked shall destroy the righteous.

17 Wherefore, he will preserve the righteous by his power, even if it so be that the fulness of his wrath must come, and the righteous be preserved, even unto the destruction of their enemies by fire. Wherefore, the righteous need not fear; for thus saith the prophet, they shall be saved, even if it so be as by fire.

18 Behold, my brethren, I say unto you, that these things must shortly come; yea, even blood, and fire, and vapor of smoke must come; and it must needs be upon the face of this earth; and it cometh unto men according to the flesh if it so be that they will harden their hearts against the Holy One of Israel.

19 For behold, the righteous shall not perish; for the time surely must come that all they who fight against Zion shall be cut off.

Date _____
☐ Completed

Date _____
☐ Completed

Date _____
☐ Completed

20 And the Lord will surely prepare a way for his people, unto the fulfilling of the words of Moses, which he spake, saying: A prophet shall the Lord your God raise up unto you, like unto me; him shall ye hear in all things whatsoever he shall say unto you. And it shall come to pass that all those who will not hear that prophet shall be cut off from among the people.

21 And now I, Nephi, declare unto you, that this prophet of whom Moses spake was the Holy One of Israel; wherefore, he shall execute judgment in righteousness.

22 And the righteous need not fear, for they are those who shall not be confounded. But it is the kingdom of the devil, which shall be built up among the children of men, which kingdom is established among them which are in the flesh—

23 For the time speedily shall come that all churches which are built up to get gain, and all those who are built up to get power over the flesh, and those who are built up to become popular in the eyes of the world, and those who seek the lusts of the flesh and the things of the world, and to do all manner of iniquity; yea, in fine, all those who belong to the kingdom of the devil are they who need fear, and tremble, and quake; they are those who must be brought low in the dust; they are those who must be consumed as stubble; and this is according to the words of the prophet.

24 And the time cometh speedily that the righteous must be led up as calves of the stall, and the Holy One of Israel must reign in dominion, and might, and power, and great glory.

25 And he gathereth his children from the four quarters of the earth; and he numbereth his sheep, and they know him; and there shall be one fold and one shepherd; and he shall feed his sheep, and in him they shall find pasture.

26 And because of the righteousness of his people, Satan has no power; wherefore, he cannot be loosed for the space of many years; for he hath no power over the hearts of the people, for they dwell in righteousness, and the Holy One of Israel reigneth.

27 And now behold, I, Nephi, say unto you that all these things must come according to the flesh.

28 But, behold, all nations, kindreds, tongues, and people shall dwell safely in the Holy One of Israel if it so be that they will repent.

29 And now I, Nephi, make an end; for I durst not speak further as yet concerning these things.

30 Wherefore, my brethren, I would that ye should consider that the things which have been written upon the plates of brass are true; and they testify that a man must be obedient to the commandments of God.

31 Wherefore, ye need not suppose that I and my father are the only ones that have testified, and also taught them. Wherefore, if ye shall be obedient to the commandments, and endure to the end, ye shall be saved at the last day. And thus it is. Amen.

Date _____
☐ Completed

Date _____
☐ Completed

Date _____
☐ Completed

2 Nephi

Chapter 1

Sight (Memorization) Words

┌─────────┐
│ **we** │
└─────────┘

Word Pattern

Pattern	-uch
Pattern words in scriptures	**much**
Location in chapter	Verse 1
Other words made from this patterns not found in chapter	such

Phonics Application

- *Words that end with vowels:* when a word ends with a vowel and it is the only vowel in the word, the vowel is usually a LONG vowel, or a vowel that says its name (example: w**e**).
- *Short vowel sounds:* the sound of the letter phonetically (versus the long sound or name of the letter). The short sound of U (example: c**u**p)
- *Consonant-Vowel-Consonant:* taking letters, phonetically saying them out loud, and bringing the sounds together to form words.
- *Blend-Vowel-Consonant:* a blend is the combination of two (or more) consonants together. These are the blends: BL, CL, FL, GL, PL, SL, BR, CR, DR, FR, GR, PR, TR, SC, SK, SM, SN, SP, ST, SW, TW.
- *Consonant Diagraphs:* diagraphs are two letters that make one sound. The diagraphs are TH, CH, SH, WH.
- *Complex Consonants:* blends that include three consonants, two consonants that sounds like a single letter, and consonant and vowel clusters.
  - *Sound alike final consonant sounds:* CH and TCH—these blends make the same sound (example: **ch**ip and wa**tch).**

Recommended (Age Appropriate) Reading Chunks

- Verses 1–5
- Verses 6–9
- Verses 10–13
- Verses 14-20
- Verses 21–25
- Verses 26–32

Gospel Principle Review/Activity

- What is the "Land of Liberty"? Does it exist now?
- *Activity:* Create a special weapon that you would need in your Armor of Righteousness. What is it for? What does it help with? (For example: a sword is often referred to as the Spirit because it helps direct the way we should go.)

Word Patterns

uch

Lesson 23: words made with –uch word pattern.
Use alphabet letters to create words.

2 Nephi 1

1 And now it came to pass that after I, Nephi, had made an end of teaching my brethren, our father, Lehi, also spake many things unto them, and rehearsed unto them, how great things the Lord had done for them in bringing them out of the land of Jerusalem.

2 And he spake unto them concerning their rebellions upon the waters, and the mercies of God in sparing their lives, that they were not swallowed up in the sea.

3 And he also spake unto them concerning the land of promise, which they had obtained—how merciful the Lord had been in warning us that we should flee out of the land of Jerusalem.

4 For, behold, said he, I have seen a vision, in which I know that Jerusalem is destroyed; and had we remained in Jerusalem we should also have perished.

5 But, said he, notwithstanding our afflictions, we have obtained a land of promise, a land which is choice above all other lands; a land which the Lord God hath covenanted with me should be a land for the inheritance of my seed. Yea, the Lord hath covenanted this land unto me, and to my children forever, and also all those who should be led out of other countries by the hand of the Lord.

6 Wherefore, I, Lehi, prophesy according to the workings of the Spirit which is in me, that there shall none come into this land save they shall be brought by the hand of the Lord.

7 Wherefore, this land is consecrated unto him whom he shall bring. And if it so be that they shall serve him according to the commandments which he hath given, it shall be a land of liberty unto them; wherefore, they shall never be brought down into captivity; if so, it shall be because of iniquity; for if iniquity shall abound cursed shall be the land for their sakes, but unto the righteous it shall be blessed forever.

8 And behold, it is wisdom that this land should be kept as yet from the knowledge of other nations; for behold, many nations would overrun the land, that there would be no place for an inheritance.

9 Wherefore, I, Lehi, have obtained a promise, that inasmuch as those whom the Lord God shall bring out of the land of Jerusalem shall keep his commandments, they shall prosper upon the face of this land; and they shall be kept from all other nations, that they may possess this land unto themselves. And if it so be that they shall keep his commandments they shall be blessed upon the face of this land, and there shall be none to molest them, nor to take away the land of their inheritance; and they shall dwell safely forever.

Date _____
☐ Completed

Date _____
☐ Completed

10 But behold, when the time cometh that they shall dwindle in unbelief, after they have received so great blessings from the hand of the Lord—having a knowledge of the creation of the earth, and all men, knowing the great and marvelous works of the Lord from the creation of the world; having power given them to do all things by faith; having all the commandments from the beginning, and having been brought by his infinite goodness into this precious land of promise—behold, I say, if the day shall come that they will reject the Holy One of Israel, the true Messiah, their Redeemer and their God, behold, the judgments of him that is just shall rest upon them.

11 Yea, he will bring other nations unto them, and he will give unto them power, and he will take away from them the lands of their possessions, and he will cause them to be scattered and smitten.

12 Yea, as one generation passeth to another there shall be bloodsheds, and great visitations among them; wherefore, my sons, I would that ye would remember; yea, I would that ye would hearken unto my words.

13 O that ye would awake; awake from a deep sleep, yea, even from the sleep of hell, and shake off the awful chains by which ye are bound, which are the chains which bind the children of men, that they are carried away captive down to the eternal gulf of misery and woe.

14 Awake! and arise from the dust, and hear the words of a trembling parent, whose limbs ye must soon lay down in the cold and silent grave, from whence no traveler can return; a few more days and I go the way of all the earth.

15 But behold, the Lord hath redeemed my soul from hell; I have beheld his glory, and I am encircled about eternally in the arms of his love.

16 And I desire that ye should remember to observe the statutes and the judgments of the Lord; behold, this hath been the anxiety of my soul from the beginning.

17 My heart hath been weighed down with sorrow from time to time, for I have feared, lest for the hardness of your hearts the Lord your God should come out in the fulness of his wrath upon you, that ye be cut off and destroyed forever;

18 Or, that a cursing should come upon you for the space of many generations; and ye are visited by sword, and by famine, and are hated, and are led according to the will and captivity of the devil.

19 O my sons, that these things might not come upon you, but that ye might be a choice and a favored people of the Lord. But behold, his will be done; for his ways are righteousness forever.

20 And he hath said that: Inasmuch as ye shall keep my commandments ye shall prosper in the land; but inasmuch as ye will not keep my commandments ye shall be cut off from my presence.

21 And now that my soul might have joy in you, and that my heart might leave this world with gladness because of you, that I might not be brought

Notes

Date _____
☐ Completed

Date _____
☐ Completed

down with grief and sorrow to the grave, arise from the dust, my sons, and be men, and be determined in one mind and in one heart, united in all things, that ye may not come down into captivity;

22 That ye may not be cursed with a sore cursing; and also, that ye may not incur the displeasure of a just God upon you, unto the destruction, yea, the eternal destruction of both soul and body.

23 Awake, my sons; put on the armor of righteousness. Shake off the chains with which ye are bound, and come forth out of obscurity, and arise from the dust.

24 Rebel no more against your brother, whose views have been glorious, and who hath kept the commandments from the time that we left Jerusalem; and who hath been an instrument in the hands of God, in bringing us forth into the land of promise; for were it not for him, we must have perished with hunger in the wilderness; nevertheless, ye sought to take away his life; yea, and he hath suffered much sorrow because of you.

25 And I exceedingly fear and tremble because of you, lest he shall suffer again; for behold, ye have accused him that he sought power and authority over you; but I know that he hath not sought for power nor authority over you, but he hath sought the glory of God, and your own eternal welfare.

26 And ye have murmured because he hath been plain unto you. Ye say that he hath used sharpness; ye say that he hath been angry with you; but behold, his sharpness was the sharpness of the power of the word of God, which was in him; and that which ye call anger was the truth, according to that which is in God, which he could not restrain, manifesting boldly concerning your iniquities.

27 And it must needs be that the power of God must be with him, even unto his commanding you that ye must obey. But behold, it was not he, but it was the Spirit of the Lord which was in him, which opened his mouth to utterance that he could not shut it.

28 And now my son, Laman, and also Lemuel and Sam, and also my sons who are the sons of Ishmael, behold, if ye will hearken unto the voice of Nephi ye shall not perish. And if ye will hearken unto him I leave unto you a blessing, yea, even my first blessing.

29 But if ye will not hearken unto him I take away my first blessing, yea, even my blessing, and it shall rest upon him.

30 And now, Zoram, I speak unto you: Behold, thou art the servant of Laban; nevertheless, thou hast been brought out of the land of Jerusalem, and I know that thou art a true friend unto my son, Nephi, forever.

31 Wherefore, because thou hast been faithful thy seed shall be blessed with his seed, that they dwell in prosperity long upon the face of this land; and nothing, save it shall be iniquity among them, shall harm or disturb their prosperity upon the face of this land forever.

32 Wherefore, if ye shall keep the commandments of the Lord, the Lord hath consecrated this land for the security of thy seed with the seed of my son.

Notes

Date _____
☐ Completed

Date _____
☐ Completed

2 Nephi

Chapter 2

Sight (Memorization) Words

were

Word Pattern

Pattern	-ast
Pattern words in scriptures	**last**
Location in chapter	Verses 26, 30
Exceptions to the rule	wast, east
Other words made from this patterns not found in chapter	cast, fast, hast, past, vast, blast

Phonics Application

- *Short vowel sounds:* the sound of the letter phonetically (versus the long sound or name of the letter).
  - The short sound of A (example: **a**pple)
- *Consonant-Vowel-Blend and Blend-Vowel-Blend:* these patterns are the merging together of sounds to make words. A blend is the combination of two (or more) consonants together. These are the blends: BL, CL, FL, GL, PL, SL, BR, CR, DR, FR, GR, PR, TR, SC, SK, SM, SN, SP, ST, SW, TW.
- *Consonant Diagraphs:* diagraphs are two letters that make one sound. The diagraphs are TH, CH, SH, WH.
- *Complex Consonants:* blends that include three consonants, two consonants that sounds like a single letter, and consonant and vowel clusters. The complex consonants are QU, TCH.

Recommended (Age Appropriate) Reading Chunks

- Verses 1–5
- Verses 6–10
- Verses 11–14
- Verses 15–20
- Verses 21–25
- Verses 26–30

Gospel Principle Review/Activity

- What is agency? Why does God let us have it?
- Why did Adam fall? What is the purpose of life?
- *Activity:* Verse 11 says that there is "opposition in all things." Take a clipboard and walk around your house. Record everything you can see that has an opposite reaction. (For example: When you walk, which direction does your foot push, and which direction does it make you go?)

Word Patterns

___ast

Lesson 24: words made with –ast word pattern.
Use alphabet letters to create words.

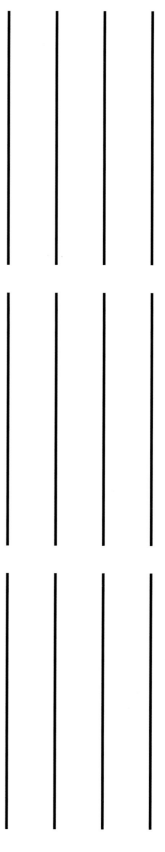

2 Nephi 2

1 And now, Jacob, I speak unto you: Thou art my first–born in the days of my tribulation in the wilderness. And behold, in thy childhood thou hast suffered afflictions and much sorrow, because of the rudeness of thy brethren.

2 Nevertheless, Jacob, my first–born in the wilderness, thou knowest the greatness of God; and he shall consecrate thine afflictions for thy gain.

3 Wherefore, thy soul shall be blessed, and thou shalt dwell safely with thy brother, Nephi; and thy days shall be spent in the service of thy God. Wherefore, I know that thou art redeemed, because of the righteousness of thy Redeemer; for thou hast beheld that in the fulness of time he cometh to bring salvation unto men.

4 And thou hast beheld in thy youth his glory; wherefore, thou art blessed even as they unto whom he shall minister in the flesh; for the Spirit is the same, yesterday, today, and forever. And the way is prepared from the fall of man, and salvation is free.

5 And men are instructed sufficiently that they know good from evil. And the law is given unto men. And by the law no flesh is justified; or, by the law men are cut off. Yea, by the temporal law they were cut off; and also, by the spiritual law they perish from that which is good, and become miserable forever.

6 Wherefore, redemption cometh in and through the Holy Messiah; for he is full of grace and truth.

7 Behold, he offereth himself a sacrifice for sin, to answer the ends of the law, unto all those who have a broken heart and a contrite spirit; and unto none else can the ends of the law be answered.

8 Wherefore, how great the importance to make these things known unto the inhabitants of the earth, that they may know that there is no flesh that can dwell in the presence of God, save it be through the merits, and mercy, and grace of the Holy Messiah, who layeth down his life according to the flesh, and taketh it again by the power of the Spirit, that he may bring to pass the resurrection of the dead, being the first that should rise.

9 Wherefore, he is the firstfruits unto God, inasmuch as he shall make intercession for all the children of men; and they that believe in him shall be saved.

10 And because of the intercession for all, all men come unto God; wherefore, they stand in the presence of him, to be judged of him according to the truth and holiness which is in him. Wherefore, the ends of the law which the Holy One hath given, unto the inflicting of the punishment which is affixed, which punishment that is affixed is in opposition to that of the happiness which is affixed, to answer the ends of the atonement—

Date _____
☐ Completed

Date _____
☐ Completed

11 For it must needs be, that there is an opposition in all things. If not so, my first-born in the wilderness, righteousness could not be brought to pass, neither wickedness, neither holiness nor misery, neither good nor bad. Wherefore, all things must needs be a compound in one; wherefore, if it should be one body it must needs remain as dead, having no life neither death, nor corruption nor incorruption, happiness nor misery, neither sense nor insensibility.

12 Wherefore, it must needs have been created for a thing of naught; wherefore there would have been no purpose in the end of its creation. Wherefore, this thing must needs destroy the wisdom of God and his eternal purposes, and also the power, and the mercy, and the justice of God.

13 And if ye shall say there is no law, ye shall also say there is no sin. If ye shall say there is no sin, ye shall also say there is no righteousness. And if there be no righteousness there be no happiness. And if there be no righteousness nor happiness there be no punishment nor misery. And if these things are not there is no God. And if there is no God we are not, neither the earth; for there could have been no creation of things, neither to act nor to be acted upon; wherefore, all things must have vanished away.

14 And now, my sons, I speak unto you these things for your profit and learning; for there is a God, and he hath created all things, both the heavens and the earth, and all things that in them are, both things to act and things to be acted upon.

---

15 And to bring about his eternal purposes in the end of man, after he had created our first parents, and the beasts of the field and the fowls of the air, and in fine, all things which are created, it must needs be that there was an opposition; even the forbidden fruit in opposition to the tree of life; the one being sweet and the other bitter.

16 Wherefore, the Lord God gave unto man that he should act for himself. Wherefore, man could not act for himself save it should be that he was enticed by the one or the other.

17 And I, Lehi, according to the things which I have read, must needs suppose that an angel of God, according to that which is written, had fallen from heaven; wherefore, he became a devil, having sought that which was evil before God.

18 And because he had fallen from heaven, and had become miserable forever, he sought also the misery of all mankind. Wherefore, he said unto Eve, yea, even that old serpent, who is the devil, who is the father of all lies, wherefore he said: Partake of the forbidden fruit, and ye shall not die, but ye shall be as God, knowing good and evil.

19 And after Adam and Eve had partaken of the forbidden fruit they were driven out of the garden of Eden, to till the earth.

20 And they have brought forth children; yea, even the family of all the earth.

Notes

Date _____
☐ Completed

Date _____
☐ Completed

21 And the days of the children of men were prolonged, according to the will of God, that they might repent while in the flesh; wherefore, their state became a state of probation, and their time was lengthened, according to the commandments which the Lord God gave unto the children of men. For he gave commandment that all men must repent; for he showed unto all men that they were lost, because of the transgression of their parents.

22 And now, behold, if Adam had not transgressed he would not have fallen, but he would have remained in the garden of Eden. And all things which were created must have remained in the same state in which they were after they were created; and they must have remained forever, and had no end.

23 And they would have had no children; wherefore they would have remained in a state of innocence, having no joy, for they knew no misery; doing no good, for they knew no sin.

24 But behold, all things have been done in the wisdom of him who knoweth all things.

25 Adam fell that men might be; and men are, that they might have joy.

26 And the Messiah cometh in the fulness of time, that he may redeem the children of men from the fall. And because that they are redeemed from the fall they have become free forever, knowing good from evil; to act for themselves and not to be acted upon, save it be by the punishment of the law at the great and last day, according to the commandments which God hath given.

27 Wherefore, men are free according to the flesh; and all things are given them which are expedient unto man. And they are free to choose liberty and eternal life, through the great Mediator of all men, or to choose captivity and death, according to the captivity and power of the devil; for he seeketh that all men might be miserable like unto himself.

28 And now, my sons, I would that ye should look to the great Mediator, and hearken unto his great commandments; and be faithful unto his words, and choose eternal life, according to the will of his Holy Spirit;

29 And not choose eternal death, according to the will of the flesh and the evil which is therein, which giveth the spirit of the devil power to captivate, to bring you down to hell, that he may reign over you in his own kingdom.

30 I have spoken these few words unto you all, my sons, in the last days of my probation; and I have chosen the good part, according to the words of the prophet. And I have none other object save it be the everlasting welfare of your souls. Amen.

Date _____
☐ Completed

Date _____
☐ Completed

2 Nephi

Chapter 3

Sight (Memorization) Words

one

Word Pattern

Pattern	-and
Pattern words in scriptures	**and, land, hand**
Location in chapter	Verses 2, 10, 15, 17
Exception to the rule	wand
Other words made from this patterns not found in chapter	band, sand, gland, brand, gran, stand

Phonics Application

- *Short vowel sounds:* the sound of the letter phonetically (versus the long sound or name of the letter).
  - The short sound of O (example: h**o**p)
- *Consonant-Vowel-Consonant:* taking letters, phonetically saying them out loud, and bringing the sounds together to form words.
- *Blend-Vowel-Consonant:* a blend is the combination of two (or more) consonants together. These are the blends: BL, CL, FL, GL, PL, SL, BR, CR, DR, FR, GR, PR, TR, SC, SK, SM, SN, SP, ST, SW, TW.
- *Consonant Diagraphs:* diagraphs are two letters that make one sound. The diagraphs are TH, CH, SH, WH.
- *Complex Consonants:* blends that include three consonants, two consonants that sounds like a single letter, and consonant and vowel clusters. The complex consonants are QU, TCH.

Recommended (Age Appropriate) Reading Chunks

- Verses 1–5
- Verses 6–11
- Verses 12–16
- Verses 17–21
- Verses 22–25

Gospel Principle Review/Activity

- What did Joseph of Egypt see in his vision?
- What are the "fruits of the loins of Judah"?
- *Activity:* Draw a picture of what you imagine Joseph saw. While you draw, have someone read what Joseph saw. Share your drawing in Family Home Evening.

Word Patterns

and

Lesson 25: words made with –and word pattern.
Use alphabet letters to create words.

2 Nephi 3

1 And now I speak unto you, Joseph, my last-born. Thou wast born in the wilderness of mine afflictions; yea, in the days of my greatest sorrow did thy mother bear thee.

2 And may the Lord consecrate also unto thee this land, which is a most precious land, for thine inheritance and the inheritance of thy seed with thy brethren, for thy security forever, if it so be that ye shall keep the commandments of the Holy One of Israel.

3 And now, Joseph, my last-born, whom I have brought out of the wilderness of mine afflictions, may the Lord bless thee forever, for thy seed shall not utterly be destroyed.

4 For behold, thou art the fruit of my loins; and I am a descendant of Joseph who was carried captive into Egypt. And great were the covenants of the Lord which he made unto Joseph.

5 Wherefore, Joseph truly saw our day. And he obtained a promise of the Lord, that out of the fruit of his loins the Lord God would raise up a righteous branch unto the house of Israel; not the Messiah, but a branch which was to be broken off, nevertheless, to be remembered in the covenants of the Lord that the Messiah should be made manifest unto them in the latter days, in the spirit of power, unto the bringing of them out of darkness unto light—yea, out of hidden darkness and out of captivity unto freedom.

Date _____
☐ Completed

6 For Joseph truly testified, saying: A seer shall the Lord my God raise up, who shall be a choice seer unto the fruit of my loins.

7 Yea, Joseph truly said: Thus saith the Lord unto me: A choice seer will I raise up out of the fruit of thy loins; and he shall be esteemed highly among the fruit of thy loins. And unto him will I give commandment that he shall do a work for the fruit of thy loins, his brethren, which shall be of great worth unto them, even to the bringing of them to the knowledge of the covenants which I have made with thy fathers.

8 And I will give unto him a commandment that he shall do none other work, save the work which I shall command him. And I will make him great in mine eyes; for he shall do my work.

9 And he shall be great like unto Moses, whom I have said I would raise up unto you, to deliver my people, O house of Israel.

10 And Moses will I raise up, to deliver thy people out of the land of Egypt.

11 But a seer will I raise up out of the fruit of thy loins; and unto him will I give power to bring forth my word unto the seed of thy loins—and not to the bringing forth my word only, saith the Lord, but to the convincing them of my word, which shall have already gone forth among them.

Date _____
☐ Completed

12 Wherefore, the fruit of thy loins shall write; and the fruit of the loins of Judah shall write; and that which shall be written by the fruit of thy loins, and also that which shall be written by the fruit of the loins of Judah, shall grow together, unto the confounding of false doctrines and laying down of contentions, and establishing peace among the fruit of thy loins, and bringing them to the knowledge of their fathers in the latter days, and also to the knowledge of my covenants, saith the Lord.

13 And out of weakness he shall be made strong, in that day when my work shall commence among all my people, unto the restoring thee, O house of Israel, saith the Lord.

14 And thus prophesied Joseph, saying: Behold, that seer will the Lord bless; and they that seek to destroy him shall be confounded; for this promise, which I have obtained of the Lord, of the fruit of my loins, shall be fulfilled. Behold, I am sure of the fulfilling of this promise;

15 And his name shall be called after me; and it shall be after the name of his father. And he shall be like unto me; for the thing, which the Lord shall bring forth by his hand, by the power of the Lord shall bring my people unto salvation.

16 Yea, thus prophesied Joseph: I am sure of this thing, even as I am sure of the promise of Moses; for the Lord hath said unto me, I will preserve thy seed forever.

17 And the Lord hath said: I will raise up a Moses; and I will give power unto him in a rod; and I will give judgment unto him in writing. Yet I will not loose his tongue, that he shall speak much, for I will not make him mighty in speaking. But I will write unto him my law, by the finger of mine own hand; and I will make a spokesman for him.

18 And the Lord said unto me also: I will raise up unto the fruit of thy loins; and I will make for him a spokesman. And I, behold, I will give unto him that he shall write the writing of the fruit of thy loins, unto the fruit of thy loins; and the spokesman of thy loins shall declare it.

19 And the words which he shall write shall be the words which are expedient in my wisdom should go forth unto the fruit of thy loins. And it shall be as if the fruit of thy loins had cried unto them from the dust; for I know their faith.

20 And they shall cry from the dust; yea, even repentance unto their brethren, even after many generations have gone by them. And it shall come to pass that their cry shall go, even according to the simpleness of their words.

21 Because of their faith their words shall proceed forth out of my mouth unto their brethren who are the fruit of thy loins; and the weakness of their words will I make strong in their faith, unto the remembering of my covenant which I made unto thy fathers.

Notes

Date _____
☐ Completed

Date _____
☐ Completed

22 And now, behold, my son Joseph, after this manner did my father of old prophesy.

23 Wherefore, because of this covenant thou art blessed; for thy seed shall not be destroyed, for they shall hearken unto the words of the book.

24 And there shall rise up one mighty among them, who shall do much good, both in word and in deed, being an instrument in the hands of God, with exceeding faith, to work mighty wonders, and do that thing which is great in the sight of God, unto the bringing to pass much restoration unto the house of Israel, and unto the seed of thy brethren.

25 And now, blessed art thou, Joseph. Behold, thou art little; wherefore hearken unto the words of thy brother, Nephi, and it shall be done unto thee even according to the words which I have spoken. Remember the words of thy dying father. Amen.

2 Nephi

Chapter 4

Sight (Memorization) Words

who

Word Pattern

Pattern	-ath
Pattern words in scriptures	**hath, path**
Location in chapter	Verses 1, 4, 20–23, 25–26, 32–33
Other words made from this patterns not found in chapter	bath, math, wrtah

Phonics Application

- *Short vowel sounds:* the sound of the letter phonetically (versus the long sound or name of the letter).
  - The short sound of A (example: **a**pple)
- *Consonant-Vowel-Consonant:* taking letters, phonetically saying them out loud, and bringing the sounds together to form words.
- *Blend-Vowel-Consonant:* a blend is the combination of two (or more) consonants together. These are the blends: BL, CL, FL, GL, PL, SL, BR, CR, DR, FR, GR, PR, TR, SC, SK, SM, SN, SP, ST, SW, TW.
- *Consonant Diagraphs:* diagraphs are two letters that make one sound. The diagraphs are TH, CH, SH, WH.
- *Complex Consonants:* blends that include three consonants, two consonants that sounds like a single letter, and consonant and vowel clusters. The complex consonants are QU, TCH.

Recommended (Age Appropriate) Reading Chunks

- Verses 1–6
- Verses 7–12
- Verses 13–20
- Verses 21–28
- Verses 29–35

Gospel Principle Review/Activity

- How do you think Nephi feltt when Lehi died?
- Why is Nephi so sad?
- *Activity:* If they had tombstones back then, what do you think Lehi's tombstone would have said?

Word Patterns

_ath

Lesson 26: words made with –ath word pattern.
Use alphabet letters to create words.

2 Nephi 4

1 And now, I, Nephi, speak concerning the prophecies of which my father hath spoken, concerning Joseph, who was carried into Egypt.

2 For behold, he truly prophesied concerning all his seed. And the prophecies which he wrote, there are not many greater. And he prophesied concerning us, and our future generations; and they are written upon the plates of brass.

3 Wherefore, after my father had made an end of speaking concerning the prophecies of Joseph, he called the children of Laman, his sons, and his daughters, and said unto them: Behold, my sons, and my daughters, who are the sons and the daughters of my first-born, I would that ye should give ear unto my words.

4 For the Lord God hath said that: Inasmuch as ye shall keep my commandments ye shall prosper in the land; and inasmuch as ye will not keep my commandments ye shall be cut off from my presence.

5 But behold, my sons and my daughters, I cannot go down to my grave save I should leave a blessing upon you; for behold, I know that if ye are brought up in the way ye should go ye will not depart from it.

6 Wherefore, if ye are cursed, behold, I leave my blessing upon you, that the cursing may be taken from you and be answered upon the heads of your parents.

7 Wherefore, because of my blessing the Lord God will not suffer that ye shall perish; wherefore, he will be merciful unto you and unto your seed forever.

8 And it came to pass that after my father had made an end of speaking to the sons and daughters of Laman, he caused the sons and daughters of Lemuel to be brought before him.

9 And he spake unto them, saying: Behold, my sons and my daughters, who are the sons and the daughters of my second son; behold I leave unto you the same blessing which I left unto the sons and daughters of Laman; wherefore, thou shalt not utterly be destroyed; but in the end thy seed shall be blessed.

10 And it came to pass that when my father had made an end of speaking unto them, behold, he spake unto the sons of Ishmael, yea, and even all his household.

11 And after he had made an end of speaking unto them, he spake unto Sam, saying: Blessed art thou, and thy seed; for thou shalt inherit the land like unto thy brother Nephi. And thy seed shall be numbered with his seed; and thou shalt be even like unto thy brother, and thy seed like unto his seed; and thou shalt be blessed in all thy days.

12 And it came to pass after my father, Lehi, had spoken unto all his household, according to the feelings of his heart and the Spirit of the Lord which was in him, he waxed old. And it came to pass that he died, and was buried.

13 And it came to pass that not many days after his death, Laman and Lemuel and the sons of Ishmael were angry with me because of the admonitions of the Lord.

14 For I, Nephi, was constrained to speak unto them, according to his word; for I had spoken many things unto them, and also my father, before his death; many of which sayings are written upon mine other plates; for a more history part are written upon mine other plates.

15 And upon these I write the things of my soul, and many of the scriptures which are engraven upon the plates of brass. For my soul delighteth in the scriptures, and my heart pondereth them, and writeth them for the learning and the profit of my children.

16 Behold, my soul delighteth in the things of the Lord; and my heart pondereth continually upon the things which I have seen and heard.

17 Nevertheless, notwithstanding the great goodness of the Lord, in showing me his great and marvelous works, my heart exclaimeth: O wretched man that I am! Yea, my heart sorroweth because of my flesh; my soul grieveth because of mine iniquities.

18 I am encompassed about, because of the temptations and the sins which do so easily beset me.

19 And when I desire to rejoice, my heart groaneth because of my sins; nevertheless, I know in whom I have trusted.

20 My God hath been my support; he hath led me through mine afflictions in the wilderness; and he hath preserved me upon the waters of the great deep.

21 He hath filled me with his love, even unto the consuming of my flesh.

22 He hath confounded mine enemies, unto the causing of them to quake before me.

23 Behold, he hath heard my cry by day, and he hath given me knowledge by visions in the night-time.

24 And by day have I waxed bold in mighty prayer before him; yea, my voice have I sent up on high; and angels came down and ministered unto me.

25 And upon the wings of his Spirit hath my body been carried away upon exceedingly high mountains. And mine eyes have beheld great things, yea, even too great for man; therefore I was bidden that I should not write them.

26 O then, if I have seen so great things, if the Lord in his condescension unto the children of men hath visited men in so much mercy, why should my heart weep and my soul linger in the valley of sorrow, and my flesh waste away, and my strength slacken, because of mine afflictions?

27 And why should I yield to sin, because of my flesh? Yea, why should I give way to temptations, that the evil one have place in my heart to

Date _____
☐ Completed

destroy my peace and afflict my soul? Why am I angry because of mine enemy?

28 Awake, my soul! No longer droop in sin. Rejoice, O my heart, and give place no more for the enemy of my soul.

---

29 Do not anger again because of mine enemies. Do not slacken my strength because of mine afflictions.

30 Rejoice, O my heart, and cry unto the Lord, and say: O Lord, I will praise thee forever; yea, my soul will rejoice in thee, my God, and the rock of my salvation.

31 O Lord, wilt thou redeem my soul? Wilt thou deliver me out of the hands of mine enemies? Wilt thou make me that I may shake at the appearance of sin?

32 May the gates of hell be shut continually before me, because that my heart is broken and my spirit is contrite! O Lord, wilt thou not shut the gates of thy righteousness before me, that I may walk in the path of the low valley, that I may be strict in the plain road!

33 O Lord, wilt thou encircle me around in the robe of thy righteousness! O Lord, wilt thou make a way for mine escape before mine enemies! Wilt thou make my path straight before me! Wilt thou not place a stumbling block in my way—but that thou wouldst clear my way before me, and hedge not up my way, but the ways of mine enemy.

34 O Lord, I have trusted in thee, and I will trust in thee forever. I will not put my trust in the arm of flesh; for I know that cursed is he that putteth his trust in the arm of flesh. Yea, cursed is he that putteth his trust in man or maketh flesh his arm.

35 Yea, I know that God will give liberally to him that asketh. Yea, my God will give me, if I ask not amiss; therefore I will lift up my voice unto thee; yea, I will cry unto thee, my God, the rock of my righteousness. Behold, my voice shall forever ascend up unto thee, my rock and mine everlasting God. Amen.

Notes

Date _____
☐ Completed

Date _____
☐ Completed

123

2 Nephi

Chapter 5

Sight (Memorization) Words

(Also: bind, blind, find, grind, mind, wind—see rule in Phonics Application.)

Word Pattern

Pattern	-ent
Pattern words in scriptures	**went**
Location in chapter	Verse 31
Exception to the rule	meant
Other words made from this patterns not found in chapter	bent, dent, lent, rent, sent, tent, vent, spent

Phonics Application

- *Rule:* most of the time, the pattern -IND, has a long I sound (see 2 Nephi 17 for the short vowel pattern word).
- *Consonant-Vowel-Consonant:* taking letters, phonetically saying them out loud, and bringing the sounds together to form words.
- *Blend-Vowel-Consonant:* a blend is the combination of two (or more) consonants together. These are the blends: BL, CL, FL, GL, PL, SL, BR, CR, DR, FR, GR, PR, TR, SC, SK, SM, SN, SP, ST, SW, TW.
- *Consonant Diagraphs:* diagraphs are two letters that make one sound. The diagraphs are TH, CH, SH, WH.
- *Complex Consonants:* blends that include three consonants, two consonants that sounds like a single letter, and consonant and vowel clusters. The complex consonants are QU, TCH.

Recommended (Age Appropriate) Reading Chunks

- Verses 1–7
- Verses 8–14
- Verses 15–20
- Verses 21–28
- Verses 29–34

Gospel Principle Review/Activity

- Why did Nephi decide to leave Laman and Lemuel? Was this a good thing?
- *Activity:* Nephi and his people built a temple. Take some sugar cubes and see if you can build a temple.
  - How would you construct it?
  - Do you think Nephi's temple looks different from ours?

Word Patterns

___ent

Lesson 27: words made with –ent word pattern.
Use alphabet letters to create words.

2 Nephi 5

1 Behold, it came to pass that I, Nephi, did cry much unto the Lord my God, because of the anger of my brethren.

2 But behold, their anger did increase against me, insomuch that they did seek to take away my life.

3 Yea, they did murmur against me, saying: Our younger brother thinks to rule over us; and we have had much trial because of him; wherefore, now let us slay him, that we may not be afflicted more because of his words. For behold, we will not have him to be our ruler; for it belongs unto us, who are the elder brethren, to rule over this people.

4 Now I do not write upon these plates all the words which they murmured against me. But it sufficeth me to say, that they did seek to take away my life.

5 And it came to pass that the Lord did warn me, that I, Nephi, should depart from them and flee into the wilderness, and all those who would go with me.

6 Wherefore, it came to pass that I, Nephi, did take my family, and also Zoram and his family, and Sam, mine elder brother and his family, and Jacob and Joseph, my younger brethren, and also my sisters, and all those who would go with me. And all those who would go with me were those who believed in the warnings and the revelations of God; wherefore, they did hearken unto my words.

7 And we did take our tents and whatsoever things were possible for us, and did journey in the wilderness for the space of many days. And after we had journeyed for the space of many days we did pitch our tents.

8 And my people would that we should call the name of the place Nephi; wherefore, we did call it Nephi.

9 And all those who were with me did take upon them to call themselves the people of Nephi.

10 And we did observe to keep the judgments, and the statutes, and the commandments of the Lord in all things, according to the law of Moses.

11 And the Lord was with us; and we did prosper exceedingly; for we did sow seed, and we did reap again in abundance. And we began to raise flocks, and herds, and animals of every kind.

12 And I, Nephi, had also brought the records which were engraven upon the plates of brass; and also the ball, or compass, which was prepared for my father by the hand of the Lord, according to that which is written.

13 And it came to pass that we began to prosper exceedingly, and to multiply in the land.

14 And I, Nephi, did take the sword of Laban, and after the manner of it

did make many swords, lest by any means the people who were now called Lamanites should come upon us and destroy us; for I knew their hatred towards me and my children and those who were called my people.

_____

15 And I did teach my people to build buildings, and to work in all manner of wood, and of iron, and of copper, and of brass, and of steel, and of gold, and of silver, and of precious ores, which were in great abundance.

16 And I, Nephi, did build a temple; and I did construct it after the manner of the temple of Solomon save it were not built of so many precious things; for they were not to be found upon the land, wherefore, it could not be built like unto Solomon's temple. But the manner of the construction was like unto the temple of Solomon; and the workmanship thereof was exceedingly fine.

17 And it came to pass that I, Nephi, did cause my people to be industrious, and to labor with their hands.

18 And it came to pass that they would that I should be their king. But I, Nephi, was desirous that they should have no king; nevertheless, I did for them according to that which was in my power.

19 And behold, the words of the Lord had been fulfilled unto my brethren, which he spake concerning them, that I should be their ruler and their teacher. Wherefore, I had been their ruler and their teacher, according to the commandments of the Lord, until the time they sought to take away my life.

20 Wherefore, the word of the Lord was fulfilled which he spake unto me, saying that: Inasmuch as they will not hearken unto thy words they shall be cut off from the presence of the Lord. And behold, they were cut off from his presence.

_____

21 And he had caused the cursing to come upon them, yea, even a sore cursing, because of their iniquity. For behold, they had hardened their hearts against him, that they had become like unto a flint; wherefore, as they were white, and exceedingly fair and delightsome, that they might not be enticing unto my people the Lord God did cause a skin of blackness to come upon them.

22 And thus saith the Lord God: I will cause that they shall be loathsome unto thy people, save they shall repent of their iniquities.

23 And cursed shall be the seed of him that mixeth with their seed; for they shall be cursed even with the same cursing. And the Lord spake it, and it was done.

24 And because of their cursing which was upon them they did become an idle people, full of mischief and subtlety, and did seek in the wilderness for beasts of prey.

25 And the Lord God said unto me: They shall be a scourge unto thy seed, to stir them up in remembrance of me; and inasmuch as they will

Notes

Date _____
☐ Completed
_____
_____
_____
_____
_____
_____
_____
_____
_____
_____
_____
_____
_____
_____
_____
_____

Date _____
☐ Completed
_____
_____
_____
_____
_____
_____
_____
_____
_____
_____
_____
_____
_____
_____
_____

not remember me, and hearken unto my words, they shall scourge them even unto destruction.

26 And it came to pass that I, Nephi, did consecrate Jacob and Joseph, that they should be priests and teachers over the land of my people.

27 And it came to pass that we lived after the manner of happiness.

28 And thirty years had passed away from the time we left Jerusalem.

---

29 And I, Nephi, had kept the records upon my plates, which I had made, of my people thus far.

30 And it came to pass that the Lord God said unto me: Make other plates; and thou shalt engraven many things upon them which are good in my sight, for the profit of thy people.

31 Wherefore, I, Nephi, to be obedient to the commandments of the Lord, went and made these plates upon which I have engraven these things.

32 And I engraved that which is pleasing unto God. And if my people are pleased with the things of God they will be pleased with mine engravings which are upon these plates.

33 And if my people desire to know the more particular part of the history of my people they must search mine other plates.

34 And it sufficeth me to say that forty years had passed away, and we had already had wars and contentions with our brethren.

2 Nephi

Chapter 6

Sight (Memorization) Words

Word Pattern

Pattern	-ick
Pattern words in scriptures	**lick**
Location in chapter	Verses 7, 13
Other words made from this patterns not found in chapter	kick, Nick, pick, Rick, sick, tick, wick, click, flick, slick, brick, trick, stick, thick, quick

Phonics Application

- *Short vowel sounds:* the sound of the letter phonetically (versus the long sound or name of the letter).
  - The short sound of I (example: h**i**t)
- *Consonant-Vowel-Blend and Blend-Vowel-Blend:* these patterns are the merging together of sounds to make words. A blend is the combination of two (or more) consonants together. These are the blends: BL, CL, FL, GL, PL, SL, BR, CR, DR, FR, GR, PR, TR, SC, SK, SM, SN, SP, ST, SW, TW.
- *Consonant Diagraphs:* diagraphs are two letters that make one sound. The diagraphs are TH, CH, SH, WH.
- *Complex Consonants:* blends that include three consonants, two consonants that sounds like a single letter, and consonant and vowel clusters. The complex Consonants are QU, TCH.

Recommended (Age Appropriate) Reading Chunks

- Verses 1–5
- Verses 6–10
- Verses 11–13
- Verses 14–18

Gospel Principle Review/Activity

- What is the "latter-day restoration"? Is that happening now?
- Why does Nephi quote from Isaiah?
- *Activity:* If you were king or president, like Jacob, what would you tell your people? Write in your journal what you think is important for your children to know.

Word Patterns

_ick

Lesson 28: words made with –ick word pattern.
Use alphabet letters to create words.

2 Nephi 6

1 The words of Jacob, the brother of Nephi, which he spake unto the people of Nephi:

2 Behold, my beloved brethren, I, Jacob, having been called of God, and ordained after the manner of his holy order, and having been consecrated by my brother Nephi, unto whom ye look as a king or a protector, and on whom ye depend for safety, behold ye know that I have spoken unto you exceedingly many things.

3 Nevertheless, I speak unto you again; for I am desirous for the welfare of your souls. Yea, mine anxiety is great for you; and ye yourselves know that it ever has been. For I have exhorted you with all diligence; and I have taught you the words of my father; and I have spoken unto you concerning all things which are written, from the creation of the world.

4 And now, behold, I would speak unto you concerning things which are, and which are to come; wherefore, I will read you the words of Isaiah. And they are the words which my brother has desired that I should speak unto you. And I speak unto you for your sakes, that ye may learn and glorify the name of your God.

5 And now, the words which I shall read are they which Isaiah spake concerning all the house of Israel; wherefore, they may be likened unto you, for ye are of the house of Israel. And there are many things which have been spoken by Isaiah which may be likened unto you, because ye are of the house of Israel.

6 And now, these are the words: Thus saith the Lord God: Behold, I will lift up mine hand to the Gentiles, and set up my standard to the people; and they shall bring thy sons in their arms, and thy daughters shall be carried upon their shoulders.

7 And kings shall be thy nursing fathers, and their queens thy nursing mothers; they shall bow down to thee with their faces towards the earth, and lick up the dust of thy feet; and thou shalt know that I am the Lord; for they shall not be ashamed that wait for me.

8 And now I, Jacob, would speak somewhat concerning these words. For behold, the Lord has shown me that those who were at Jerusalem, from whence we came, have been slain and carried away captive.

9 Nevertheless, the Lord has shown unto me that they should return again. And he also has shown unto me that the Lord God, the Holy One of Israel, should manifest himself unto them in the flesh; and after he should manifest himself they should scourge him and crucify him, according to the words of the angel who spake it unto me.

10 And after they have hardened their hearts and stiffened their necks against the Holy One of Israel, behold, the judgments of the Holy One of Israel shall come upon them. And the day cometh that they shall be smitten and afflicted.

Date _____

☐ Completed

Date _____

☐ Completed

11 Wherefore, after they are driven to and fro, for thus saith the angel, many shall be afflicted in the flesh, and shall not be suffered to perish, because of the prayers of the faithful; they shall be scattered, and smitten, and hated; nevertheless, the Lord will be merciful unto them, that when they shall come to the knowledge of their Redeemer, they shall be gathered together again to the lands of their inheritance.

12 And blessed are the Gentiles, they of whom the prophet has written; for behold, if it so be that they shall repent and fight not against Zion, and do not unite themselves to that great and abominable church, they shall be saved; for the Lord God will fulfil his covenants which he has made unto his children; and for this cause the prophet has written these things.

13 Wherefore, they that fight against Zion and the covenant people of the Lord shall lick up the dust of their feet; and the people of the Lord shall not be ashamed. For the people of the Lord are they who wait for him; for they still wait for the coming of the Messiah.

14 And behold, according to the words of the prophet, the Messiah will set himself again the second time to recover them; wherefore, he will manifest himself unto them in power and great glory, unto the destruction of their enemies, when that day cometh when they shall believe in him; and none will he destroy that believe in him.

15 And they that believe not in him shall be destroyed, both by fire, and by tempest, and by earthquakes, and by bloodsheds, and by pestilence, and by famine. And they shall know that the Lord is God, the Holy One of Israel.

16 For shall the prey be taken from the mighty, or the lawful captive delivered?

17 But thus saith the Lord: Even the captives of the mighty shall be taken away, and the prey of the terrible shall be delivered; for the Mighty God shall deliver his covenant people. For thus saith the Lord: I will contend with them that contendeth with thee—

18 And I will feed them that oppress thee, with their own flesh; and they shall be drunken with their own blood as with sweet wine; and all flesh shall know that I the Lord am thy Savior and thy Redeemer, the Mighty One of Jacob.

Notes

Date _____
☐ Completed

Date _____
☐ Completed

2 Nephi

Chapter 7

Sight (Memorization) Words

Word Pattern

Pattern	-ack
Pattern words in scriptures	**back**
Location in chapter	Verses 5–6
Exception to the rule	plaque
Other words made from this patterns not found in chapter	Jack, lack, pack, rack, sack, tack, Zack, black, slack, track, smack, snack, stack, shack

Phonics Application

- *Short vowel sounds:* the sound of the letter phonetically (versus the long sound or name of the letter).
  - The short sound of A (example: **a**pple)
- *Consonant-Vowel-Blend and Blend-Vowel-Blend:* these patterns are the merging together of sounds to make words. A blend is the combination of two (or more) consonants together. These are the blends: BL, CL, FL, GL, PL, SL, BR, CR, DR, FR, GR, PR, TR, SC, SK, SM, SN, SP, ST, SW, TW.
- *Consonant Diagraphs:* diagraphs are two letters that make one sound. The diagraphs are TH, CH, SH, WH.
- *Complex Consonants:* blends that include three consonants, two consonants that sounds like a single letter, and consonant and vowel clusters. The complex consonants are QU, TCH.

Recommended (Age Appropriate) Reading Chunks

- Verses 1–5
- Verses 6–11

Gospel Principle Review/Activity

- What is the "tongue of the learned"?
- How do we "sell ourselves"?
- *Activity:* Isaiah talks about walking in the darkness and having no light. Turn off the lights (during the evening). How does the dark make you feel? Do you think you can get around without hurting yourself?

Word Patterns

ack

Lesson 29: words made with –ack word pattern.
Use alphabet letters to create words.

2 Nephi 7

1 Yea, for thus saith the Lord: Have I put thee away, or have I cast thee off forever? For thus saith the Lord: Where is the bill of your mother's divorcement? To whom have I put thee away, or to which of my creditors have I sold you? Yea, to whom have I sold you? Behold, for your iniquities have ye sold yourselves, and for your transgressions is your mother put away.

2 Wherefore, when I came, there was no man; when I called, yea, there was none to answer. O house of Israel, is my hand shortened at all that it cannot redeem, or have I no power to deliver? Behold, at my rebuke I dry up the sea, I make their rivers a wilderness and their fish to stink because the waters are dried up, and they die because of thirst.

3 I clothe the heavens with blackness, and I make sackcloth their covering.

4 The Lord God hath given me the tongue of the learned, that I should know how to speak a word in season unto thee, O house of Israel. When ye are weary he waketh morning by morning. He waketh mine ear to hear as the learned.

5 The Lord God hath opened mine ear, and I was not rebellious, neither turned away back.

---

6 I gave my back to the smiter, and my cheeks to them that plucked off the hair. I hid not my face from shame and spitting.

7 For the Lord God will help me, therefore shall I not be confounded. Therefore have I set my face like a flint, and I know that I shall not be ashamed.

8 And the Lord is near, and he justifieth me. Who will contend with me? Let us stand together. Who is mine adversary? Let him come near me, and I will smite him with the strength of my mouth.

9 For the Lord God will help me. And all they who shall condemn me, behold, all they shall wax old as a garment, and the moth shall eat them up.

10 Who is among you that feareth the Lord, that obeyeth the voice of his servant, that walketh in darkness and hath no light?

11 Behold all ye that kindle fire, that compass yourselves about with sparks, walk in the light of your fire and in the sparks which ye have kindled. This shall ye have of mine hand—ye shall lie down in sorrow.

Date _____
☐ Completed

Date _____
☐ Completed

2 Nephi

Chapter 8

Sight (Memorization) Words

Word Pattern

Pattern	-unk
Pattern words in scriptures	**drunk**
Location in chapter	Verse 17
Exception to the rule	monk
Other words made from this patterns not found in chapter	bunk, dunk, funk, hunk, junk, punk, sunk, flunk, trunk, skunk, spunk stunk

Phonics Application

- *Short vowel sounds:* the sound of the letter phonetically (versus the long sound or name of the letter).
  - The short sound of U (example: c**u**p)
- *Consonant-Vowel-Blend and Blend-Vowel-Blend:* these patterns are the merging together of sounds to make words. A blend is the combination of two (or more) consonants together. These are the blends: BL, CL, FL, GL, PL, SL, BR, CR, DR, FR, GR, PR, TR, SC, SK, SM, SN, SP, ST, SW, TW.
- *Consonant Diagraphs:* diagraphs are two letters that make one sound. The diagraphs are TH, CH, SH, WH.
- *Complex Consonants:* blends that include three consonants, two consonants that sounds like a single letter, and consonant and vowel clusters. The complex consonants are QU, TCH.

Recommended (Age Appropriate) Reading Chunks

- Verses 1–7
- Verses 8–14
- Verses 15–19
- Verses 20–25

Gospel Principle Review/Activity

- Why is Zion a place of great joy?
- *Activity:* The Lord tells us to "put on strength." What does the Lord mean when He says to be strong? How can we put on strength?
  - Gather materials around your house that you think you can "put on" to have more strength. Describe why you chose the items you did.

Word Patterns

unk

Lesson 30: words made with –unk word pattern.
Use alphabet letters to create words.

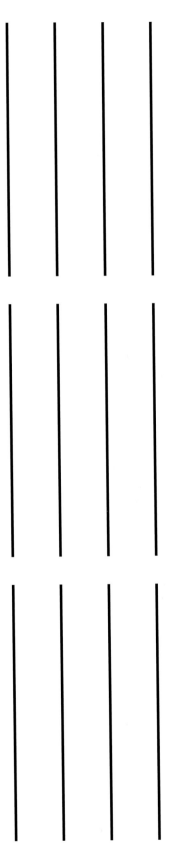

2 Nephi 8

1 Hearken unto me, ye that follow after righteousness. Look unto the rock from whence ye are hewn, and to the hole of the pit from whence ye are digged.

2 Look unto Abraham, your father, and unto Sarah, she that bare you; for I called him alone, and blessed him.

3 For the Lord shall comfort Zion, he will comfort all her waste places; and he will make her wilderness like Eden, and her desert like the garden of the Lord. Joy and gladness shall be found therein, thanksgiving and the voice of melody.

4 Hearken unto me, my people; and give ear unto me, O my nation; for a law shall proceed from me, and I will make my judgment to rest for a light for the people.

5 My righteousness is near; my salvation is gone forth, and mine arm shall judge the people. The isles shall wait upon me, and on mine arm shall they trust.

6 Lift up your eyes to the heavens, and look upon the earth beneath; for the heavens shall vanish away like smoke, and the earth shall wax old like a garment; and they that dwell therein shall die in like manner. But my salvation shall be forever, and my righteousness shall not be abolished.

7 Hearken unto me, ye that know righteousness, the people in whose heart I have written my law, fear ye not the reproach of men, neither be ye afraid of their revilings.

8 For the moth shall eat them up like a garment, and the worm shall eat them like wool. But my righteousness shall be forever, and my salvation from generation to generation.

9 Awake, awake! Put on strength, O arm of the Lord; awake as in the ancient days. Art thou not he that hath cut Rahab, and wounded the dragon?

10 Art thou not he who hath dried the sea, the waters of the great deep; that hath made the depths of the sea a way for the ransomed to pass over?

11 Therefore, the redeemed of the Lord shall return, and come with singing unto Zion; and everlasting joy and holiness shall be upon their heads; and they shall obtain gladness and joy; sorrow and mourning shall flee away.

12 I am he; yea, I am he that comforteth you. Behold, who art thou, that thou shouldst be afraid of man, who shall die, and of the son of man, who shall be made like unto grass?

13 And forgettest the Lord thy maker, that hath stretched forth the heavens, and laid the foundations of the earth, and hast feared continually every day, because of the fury of the oppressor, as if he were ready to destroy? And where is the fury of the oppressor?

14 The captive exile hasteneth, that he may be loosed, and that he

should not die in the pit, nor that his bread should fail.

15 But I am the Lord thy God, whose waves roared; the Lord of Hosts is my name.
16 And I have put my words in thy mouth, and have covered thee in the shadow of mine hand, that I may plant the heavens and lay the foundations of the earth, and say unto Zion: Behold, thou art my people.
17 Awake, awake, stand up, O Jerusalem, which hast drunk at the hand of the Lord the cup of his fury—thou hast drunken the dregs of the cup of trembling wrung out—
18 And none to guide her among all the sons she hath brought forth; neither that taketh her by the hand, of all the sons she hath brought up.
19 These two sons are come unto thee, who shall be sorry for thee—thy desolation and destruction, and the famine and the sword—and by whom shall I comfort thee?

20 Thy sons have fainted, save these two; they lie at the head of all the streets; as a wild bull in a net, they are full of the fury of the Lord, the rebuke of thy God.
21 Therefore hear now this, thou afflicted, and drunken, and not with wine:
22 Thus saith thy Lord, the Lord and thy God pleadeth the cause of his people; behold, I have taken out of thine hand the cup of trembling, the dregs of the cup of my fury; thou shalt no more drink it again.
23 But I will put it into the hand of them that afflict thee; who have said to thy soul: Bow down, that we may go over—and thou hast laid thy body as the ground and as the street to them that went over.
24 Awake, awake, put on thy strength, O Zion; put on thy beautiful garments, O Jerusalem, the holy city; for henceforth there shall no more come into thee the uncircumcised and the unclean.
25 Shake thyself from the dust; arise, sit down, O Jerusalem; loose thyself from the bands of thy neck, O captive daughter of Zion.

Date _____
☐ Completed

_____
_____
_____
_____
_____
_____
_____
_____

Date _____
☐ Completed

_____
_____
_____
_____
_____
_____
_____
_____
_____

Date _____
☐ Completed

_____
_____
_____
_____
_____
_____
_____
_____

2 Nephi

Chapter 9—Review

Sight (Memorization) Words

we	were	one	who
kind	have	put	buy

Word Pattern

Pattern	-uch, utch	-ast	-and	-ath	-ent
Pattern words reviewed	much	last	land, band	hath, path	went

Pattern	-ick	pack	-unk
Pattern words reviewed	lick	back	drunk

Phonics Application

- *Short vowel sounds:* the sound of the letter phonetically (versus the long sound or name of the letter).
  - The short sound of A (example: **a**pple)
  - The short sound of E (example: b**e**d)
  - The short sound of I (example: h**i**t)
  - The short sound of U (example: c**u**p)
- *Consonant-Vowel-Blend and Blend-Vowel-Blend:* these patterns are the merging together of sounds to make words. A blend is the combination of two (or more) consonants together. These are the blends: BL, CL, FL, GL, PL, SL, BR, CR, DR, FR, GR, PR, TR, SC, SK, SM, SN, SP, ST, SW, TW.
- *Consonant Diagraphs:* diagraphs are two letters that make one sound. The diagraphs are TH, CH, SH, WH.
- *Complex Consonants:* blends that include three consonants, two consonants that sounds like a single letter, and consonant and vowel clusters. The complex consonants are QU, TCH.

Recommended (Age Appropriate) Reading Chunks

- Verses 1–5
- Verses 6–9
- Verses 10–14
- Verses 15–18
- Verses 19–25
- Verses 26–29
- Verses 30–39
- Verses 40–43
- Verses 44–48
- Verses 49–54

Gospel Principle Review/Activity

- What is the Atonement and what are the two deaths it saves us from?
- *Activity:* Learn how Christ came into the world so that He could "save all men if they hearken unto his voice."
  - Read Matthew 26–28 in the New Testament about the death of Christ and what the Atonement is.
  - Record your feelings about Jesus Christ's sacrifice in your journal.

Word Patterns—Review

Lesson 31 Review: Find the words in the word box in the word search.

Word Box

much	
last	
sand	
hath	
went	
pick	
tack	
dunk	

```
H T O E F E A K Z R
T G A P T L Y Z T M
A S M C G W S N U V
H N D K U E C Y Q
T S A L N W H F X K
D C N Y B A P I C K
U B H P U C S S C H
N T R T D I D D Q U
K X P I T A L N L Q
U C A Z M W H S H W
```

2 Nephi 9

1 And now, my beloved brethren, I have read these things that ye might know concerning the covenants of the Lord that he has covenanted with all the house of Israel—

2 That he has spoken unto the Jews, by the mouth of his holy prophets, even from the beginning down, from generation to generation, until the time comes that they shall be restored to the true church and fold of God; when they shall be gathered home to the lands of their inheritance, and shall be established in all their lands of promise.

3 Behold, my beloved brethren, I speak unto you these things that ye may rejoice, and lift up your heads forever, because of the blessings which the Lord God shall bestow upon your children.

4 For I know that ye have searched much, many of you, to know of things to come; wherefore I know that ye know that our flesh must waste away and die; nevertheless, in our bodies we shall see God.

5 Yea, I know that ye know that in the body he shall show himself unto those at Jerusalem, from whence we came; for it is expedient that it should be among them; for it behooveth the great Creator that he suffereth himself to become subject unto man in the flesh, and die for all men, that all men might become subject unto him.

Date _____
☐ Completed

6 For as death hath passed upon all men, to fulfil the merciful plan of the great Creator, there must needs be a power of resurrection, and the resurrection must needs come unto man by reason of the fall; and the fall came by reason of transgression; and because man became fallen they were cut off from the presence of the Lord.

7 Wherefore, it must needs be an infinite atonement—save it should be an infinite atonement this corruption could not put on incorruption. Wherefore, the first judgment which came upon man must needs have remained to an endless duration. And if so, this flesh must have laid down to rot and to crumble to its mother earth, to rise no more.

8 O the wisdom of God, his mercy and grace! For behold, if the flesh should rise no more our spirits must become subject to that angel who fell from before the presence of the Eternal God, and became the devil, to rise no more.

9 And our spirits must have become like unto him, and we become devils, angels to a devil, to be shut out from the presence of our God, and to remain with the father of lies, in misery, like unto himself; yea, to that being who beguiled our first parents, who transformeth himself nigh unto an angel of light, and stirreth up the children of men unto secret combinations of murder and all manner of secret works of darkness.

Date _____
☐ Completed

10 O how great the goodness of our God, who prepareth a way for our escape from the grasp of this awful monster; yea, that monster, death and hell, which I call the death of the body, and also the death of the spirit.

11 And because of the way of deliverance of our God, the Holy One of Israel, this death, of which I have spoken, which is the temporal, shall deliver up its dead; which death is the grave.

12 And this death of which I have spoken, which is the spiritual death, shall deliver up its dead; which spiritual death is hell; wherefore, death and hell must deliver up their dead, and hell must deliver up its captive spirits, and the grave must deliver up its captive bodies, and the bodies and the spirits of men will be restored one to the other; and it is by the power of the resurrection of the Holy One of Israel.

13 O how great the plan of our God! For on the other hand, the paradise of God must deliver up the spirits of the righteous, and the grave deliver up the body of the righteous; and the spirit and the body is restored to itself again, and all men become incorruptible, and immortal, and they are living souls, having a perfect knowledge like unto us in the flesh, save it be that our knowledge shall be perfect.

14 Wherefore, we shall have a perfect knowledge of all our guilt, and our uncleanness, and our nakedness; and the righteous shall have a perfect knowledge of their enjoyment, and their righteousness, being clothed with purity, yea, even with the robe of righteousness.

---

15 And it shall come to pass that when all men shall have passed from this first death unto life, insomuch as they have become immortal, they must appear before the judgment-seat of the Holy One of Israel; and then cometh the judgment, and then must they be judged according to the holy judgment of God.

16 And assuredly, as the Lord liveth, for the Lord God hath spoken it, and it is his eternal word, which cannot pass away, that they who are righteous shall be righteous still, and they who are filthy shall be filthy still; wherefore, they who are filthy are the devil and his angels; and they shall go away into everlasting fire, prepared for them; and their torment is as a lake of fire and brimstone, whose flame ascendeth up forever and ever and has no end.

17 O the greatness and the justice of our God! For he executeth all his words, and they have gone forth out of his mouth, and his law must be fulfilled.

18 But, behold, the righteous, the saints of the Holy One of Israel, they who have believed in the Holy One of Israel, they who have endured the crosses of the world, and despised the shame of it, they shall inherit the kingdom of God, which was prepared for them from the foundation of the world, and their joy shall be full forever.

19 O the greatness of the mercy of our God, the Holy One of Israel! For he delivereth his saints from that awful monster the devil, and death, and hell, and that lake of fire and brimstone, which is endless torment.

20 O how great the holiness of our God! For he knoweth all things, and there is not anything save he knows it.

21 And he cometh into the world that he may save all men if they will hearken unto his voice; for behold, he suffereth the pains of all men, yea, the pains of every living creature, both men, women, and children, who belong to the family of Adam.

22 And he suffereth this that the resurrection might pass upon all men, that all might stand before him at the great and judgment day.

23 And he commandeth all men that they must repent, and be baptized in his name, having perfect faith in the Holy One of Israel, or they cannot be saved in the kingdom of God.

24 And if they will not repent and believe in his name, and be baptized in his name, and endure to the end, they must be damned; for the Lord God, the Holy One of Israel, has spoken it.

25 Wherefore, he has given a law; and where there is no law given there is no punishment; and where there is no punishment there is no condemnation; and where there is no condemnation the mercies of the Holy One of Israel have claim upon them, because of the atonement; for they are delivered by the power of him.

26 For the atonement satisfieth the demands of his justice upon all those who have not the law given to them, that they are delivered from that awful monster, death and hell, and the devil, and the lake of fire and brimstone, which is endless torment; and they are restored to that God who gave them breath, which is the Holy One of Israel.

27 But wo unto him that has the law given, yea, that has all the commandments of God, like unto us, and that transgresseth them, and that wasteth the days of his probation, for awful is his state!

28 O that cunning plan of the evil one! O the vainness, and the frailties, and the foolishness of men! When they are learned they think they are wise, and they hearken not unto the counsel of God, for they set it aside, supposing they know of themselves, wherefore, their wisdom is foolishness and it profiteth them not. And they shall perish.

29 But to be learned is good if they hearken unto the counsels of God.

30 But wo unto the rich, who are rich as to the things of the world. For because they are rich they despise the poor, and they persecute the meek, and their hearts are upon their treasures; wherefore, their treasure is their God. And behold, their treasure shall perish with them also.

31 And wo unto the deaf that will not hear; for they shall perish.

32 Wo unto the blind that will not see; for they shall perish also.

Date _____
☐ Completed

Date _____
☐ Completed

33 Wo unto the uncircumcised of heart, for a knowledge of their iniquities shall smite them at the last day.

34 Wo unto the liar, for he shall be thrust down to hell.

35 Wo unto the murderer who deliberately killeth, for he shall die.

36 Wo unto them who commit whoredoms, for they shall be thrust down to hell.

37 Yea, wo unto those that worship idols, for the devil of all devils delighteth in them.

38 And, in fine, wo unto all those who die in their sins; for they shall return to God, and behold his face, and remain in their sins.

39 O, my beloved brethren, remember the awfulness in transgressing against that Holy God, and also the awfulness of yielding to the enticings of that cunning one. Remember, to be carnally–minded is death, and to be spiritually–minded is life eternal.

_____

40 O, my beloved brethren, give ear to my words. Remember the greatness of the Holy One of Israel. Do not say that I have spoken hard things against you; for if ye do, ye will revile against the truth; for I have spoken the words of your Maker. I know that the words of truth are hard against all uncleanness; but the righteous fear them not, for they love the truth and are not shaken.

41 O then, my beloved brethren, come unto the Lord, the Holy One. Remember that his paths are righteous. Behold, the way for man is narrow, but it lieth in a straight course before him, and the keeper of the gate is the Holy One of Israel; and he employeth no servant there; and there is none other way save it be by the gate; for he cannot be deceived, for the Lord God is his name.

42 And whoso knocketh, to him will he open; and the wise, and the learned, and they that are rich, who are puffed up because of their learning, and their wisdom, and their riches—yea, they are they whom he despiseth; and save they shall cast these things away, and consider themselves fools before God, and come down in the depths of humility, he will not open unto them.

43 But the things of the wise and the prudent shall be hid from them forever—yea, that happiness which is prepared for the saints.

_____

44 O, my beloved brethren, remember my words. Behold, I take off my garments, and I shake them before you; I pray the God of my salvation that he view me with his all–searching eye; wherefore, ye shall know at the last day, when all men shall be judged of their works, that the God of Israel did witness that I shook your iniquities from my soul, and that I stand with brightness before him, and am rid of your blood.

45 O, my beloved brethren, turn away from your sins; shake off the chains of him that would bind you fast; come unto that God who is the rock of your salvation.

46 Prepare your souls for that glorious day when justice shall be administered unto the righteous, even the day of judgment, that ye may not shrink with awful fear; that ye may not remember your awful guilt in perfectness, and be constrained to exclaim: Holy, holy are thy judgments, O Lord God Almighty—but I know my guilt; I transgressed thy law, and my transgressions are mine; and the devil hath obtained me, that I am a prey to his awful misery.

47 But behold, my brethren, is it expedient that I should awake you to an awful reality of these things? Would I harrow up your souls if your minds were pure? Would I be plain unto you according to the plainness of the truth if ye were freed from sin?

48 Behold, if ye were holy I would speak unto you of holiness; but as ye are not holy, and ye look upon me as a teacher, it must needs be expedient that I teach you the consequences of sin.

49 Behold, my soul abhorreth sin, and my heart delighteth in righteousness; and I will praise the holy name of my God.

50 Come, my brethren, every one that thirsteth, come ye to the waters; and he that hath no money, come buy and eat; yea, come buy wine and milk without money and without price.

51 Wherefore, do not spend money for that which is of no worth, nor your labor for that which cannot satisfy. Hearken diligently unto me, and remember the words which I have spoken; and come unto the Holy One of Israel, and feast upon that which perisheth not, neither can be corrupted, and let your soul delight in fatness.

52 Behold, my beloved brethren, remember the words of your God; pray unto him continually by day, and give thanks unto his holy name by night. Let your hearts rejoice.

53 And behold how great the covenants of the Lord, and how great his condescensions unto the children of men; and because of his greatness, and his grace and mercy, he has promised unto us that our seed shall not utterly be destroyed, according to the flesh, but that he would preserve them; and in future generations they shall become a righteous branch unto the house of Israel.

54 And now, my brethren, I would speak unto you more; but on the morrow I will declare unto you the remainder of my words. Amen.

Date _____
☐ Completed

Date _____
☐ Completed

2 Nephi

Chapter 10

Sight (Memorization) Words

says

(Note: only "says" does not follow learned phonics rules; "say" and other word forms, initially taught in Mosiah 1, will be highlighted.)

Word Pattern

Pattern	-ond
Pattern words in scriptures	**bond**
Location in chapter	Verse 16
Exception to the rule	wand
Other words made from this patterns not found in chapter	fond, pond, blond

Phonics Application

- *Short vowel sounds:* the sound of the letter phonetically (versus the long sound or name of the letter).
  - The short sound of O (example: h**o**p)
- *Consonant-Vowel-Blend and Blend-Vowel-Blend:* these patterns are the merging together of sounds to make words. A blend is the combination of two (or more) consonants together. These are the blends: BL, CL, FL, GL, PL, SL, BR, CR, DR, FR, GR, PR, TR, SC, SK, SM, SN, SP, ST, SW, TW.
- *Consonant Diagraphs:* diagraphs are two letters that make one sound. The diagraphs are TH, CH, SH, WH.
- *Complex Consonants:* blends that include three consonants, two consonants that sounds like a single letter, and consonant and vowel clusters. The complex consonants are QU, TCH.

Recommended (Age Appropriate) Reading Chunks

- Verses 1–6
- Verses 7–13
- Verses 14–19
- Verses 20–25

Gospel Principle Review/Activity

- Who is speaking in this chapter? How is he related to Nephi?
- Why did the Jews crucify Jesus Christ?
- *Activity:* After telling us some hard and sad things, the Lord tells us to "cheer up [our] hearts." Make a list of ways you can cheer up your heart when you are feeling sad.
  - Does the Lord want us to be happy?
  - How can you be like Jesus and try to make other people happy?

Word Patterns

___ond

Lesson 32: words made with –ond word pattern.
Use alphabet letters to create words.

2 Nephi 10

1 And now I, Jacob, speak unto you again, my beloved brethren, concerning this righteous branch of which I have spoken.

2 For behold, the promises which we have obtained are promises unto us according to the flesh; wherefore, as it has been shown unto me that many of our children shall perish in the flesh because of unbelief, nevertheless, God will be merciful unto many; and our children shall be restored, that they may come to that which will give them the true knowledge of their Redeemer.

3 Wherefore, as I said unto you, it must needs be expedient that Christ—for in the last night the angel spake unto me that this should be his name—should come among the Jews, among those who are the more wicked part of the world; and they shall crucify him—for thus it behooveth our God, and there is none other nation on earth that would crucify their God.

4 For should the mighty miracles be wrought among other nations they would repent, and know that he be their God.

5 But because of priestcrafts and iniquities, they at Jerusalem will stiffen their necks against him, that he be crucified.

6 Wherefore, because of their iniquities, destructions, famines, pestilences, and bloodshed shall come upon them; and they who shall not be destroyed shall be scattered among all nations.

7 But behold, thus saith the Lord God: When the day cometh that they shall believe in me, that I am Christ, then have I covenanted with their fathers that they shall be restored in the flesh, upon the earth, unto the lands of their inheritance.

8 And it shall come to pass that they shall be gathered in from their long dispersion, from the isles of the sea, and from the four parts of the earth; and the nations of the Gentiles shall be great in the eyes of me, saith God, in carrying them forth to the lands of their inheritance.

9 Yea, the kings of the Gentiles shall be nursing fathers unto them, and their queens shall become nursing mothers; wherefore, the promises of the Lord are great unto the Gentiles, for he hath spoken it, and who can dispute?

10 But behold, this land, said God, shall be a land of thine inheritance, and the Gentiles shall be blessed upon the land.

11 And this land shall be a land of liberty unto the Gentiles, and there shall be no kings upon the land, who shall raise up unto the Gentiles.

12 And I will fortify this land against all other nations.

13 And he that fighteth against Zion shall perish, saith God.

14 For he that raiseth up a king against me shall perish, for I, the Lord, the king of heaven, will be their king, and I will be a light unto them forever, that hear my words.

15 Wherefore, for this cause, that my covenants may be fulfilled which I have made unto the children of men, that I will do unto them while they are in the flesh, I must needs destroy the secret works of darkness, and of murders, and of abominations.

16 Wherefore, he that fighteth against Zion, both Jew and Gentile, both bond and free, both male and female, shall perish; for they are they who are the whore of all the earth; for they who are not for me are against me, saith our God.

17 For I will fulfil my promises which I have made unto the children of men, that I will do unto them while they are in the flesh—

18 Wherefore, my beloved brethren, thus saith our God: I will afflict thy seed by the hand of the Gentiles; nevertheless, I will soften the hearts of the Gentiles, that they shall be like unto a father to them; wherefore, the Gentiles shall be blessed and numbered among the house of Israel.

19 Wherefore, I will consecrate this land unto thy seed, and them who shall be numbered among thy seed, forever, for the land of their inheritance; for it is a choice land, saith God unto me, above all other lands, wherefore I will have all men that dwell thereon that they shall worship me, saith God.

20 And now, my beloved brethren, seeing that our merciful God has given us so great knowledge concerning these things, let us remember him, and lay aside our sins, and not hang down our heads, for we are not cast off; nevertheless, we have been driven out of the land of our inheritance; but we have been led to a better land, for the Lord has made the sea our path, and we are upon an isle of the sea.

21 But great are the promises of the Lord unto them who are upon the isles of the sea; wherefore as it says isles, there must needs be more than this, and they are inhabited also by our brethren.

22 For behold, the Lord God has led away from time to time from the house of Israel, according to his will and pleasure. And now behold, the Lord remembereth all them who have been broken off, wherefore he remembereth us also.

23 Therefore, cheer up your hearts, and remember that ye are free to act for yourselves—to choose the way of everlasting death or the way of eternal life.

24 Wherefore, my beloved brethren, reconcile yourselves to the will of God, and not to the will of the devil and the flesh; and remember, after ye are reconciled unto God, that it is only in and through the grace of God that ye are saved.

25 Wherefore, may God raise you from death by the power of the resurrection, and also from everlasting death by the power of the atonement, that ye may be received into the eternal kingdom of God, that ye may praise him through grace divine. Amen.

Notes

Date _____
☐ Completed

Date _____
☐ Completed

2 Nephi

Chapter 11

Sight (Memorization) Words

also

Word Pattern

Pattern	-ill
Pattern words in scriptures	**will**
Location in chapter	Verses 2–3
Other words made from this patterns not found in chapter	Bill, dill, fill, hill, Jill, kill, pill, till, drill, frill, grill, spill, still

Phonics Application

- *Short vowel sounds:* the sound of the letter phonetically (versus the long sound or name of the letter).
  - The short sound of I (example: h**i**t)
- *Consonant-Vowel-Blend and Blend-Vowel-Blend:* these patterns are the merging together of sounds to make words. A blend is the combination of two (or more) consonants together. These are the blends: BL, CL, FL, GL, PL, SL, BR, CR, DR, FR, GR, PR, TR, SC, SK, SM, SN, SP, ST, SW, TW.
- *Consonant Diagraphs:* diagraphs are two letters that make one sound. The diagraphs are TH, CH, SH, WH.
- *Complex Consonants:* blends that include three consonants, two consonants that sounds like a single letter, and consonant and vowel clusters. The complex consonants are QU, TCH.
- *Doublet:* a special type of across-syllable pattern in which the two consonants are the same.
  - LL (example: ba**ll**)

Recommended (Age Appropriate) Reading Chunks

- Verses 1–8

Gospel Principle Review/Activity

- Who did Jacob see?
- *Activity:* There have been many people who have tried to draw what Jesus looks like. What do you imagine Jesus' face to look like? Draw what you think Jesus looks like.

Word Patterns

ill

Lesson 33: words made with –ill word pattern.
Use alphabet letters to create words.

2 Nephi 11

1 And now, Jacob spake many more things to my people at that time; nevertheless only these things have I caused to be written, for the things which I have written sufficeth me.

2 And now I, Nephi, write more of the words of Isaiah, for my soul delighteth in his words. For I will liken his words unto my people, and I will send them forth unto all my children, for he verily saw my Redeemer, even as I have seen him.

3 And my brother, Jacob, also has seen him as I have seen him; wherefore, I will send their words forth unto my children to prove unto them that my words are true. Wherefore, by the words of three, God hath said, I will establish my word. Nevertheless, God sendeth more witnesses, and he proveth all his words.

4 Behold, my soul delighteth in proving unto my people the truth of the coming of Christ; for, for this end hath the law of Moses been given; and all things which have been given of God from the beginning of the world, unto man, are the typifying of him.

5 And also my soul delighteth in the covenants of the Lord which he hath made to our fathers; yea, my soul delighteth in his grace, and in his justice, and power, and mercy in the great and eternal plan of deliverance from death.

6 And my soul delighteth in proving unto my people that save Christ should come all men must perish.

7 For if there be no Christ there be no God; and if there be no God we are not, for there could have been no creation. But there is a God, and he is Christ, and he cometh in the fulness of his own time.

8 And now I write some of the words of Isaiah, that whoso of my people shall see these words may lift up their hearts and rejoice for all men. Now these are the words, and ye may liken them unto you and unto all men.

Date _____

☐ Completed

2 Nephi

Chapter 12

Sight (Memorization) Words

gold

(Also old, fold, hold, sold, told—see the rule in Phonics Application.)

Word Pattern

Pattern	-ock
Pattern words in scriptures	**rock, rocks**
Location in chapter	Verse 10
Exceptions to the rule	knock, walk
Other words made from this patterns not found in chapter	dock, jock, lock, mock, sock, tock, block, flock, smock, stock, shock

Phonics Application

- *Short vowel sounds:* the sound of the letter phonetically (versus the long sound or name of the letter).
  - The short sound of O (example: h**o**p)
- *Consonant-Vowel-Blend and Blend-Vowel-Blend:* these patterns are the merging together of sounds to make words. A blend is the combination of two (or more) consonants together. These are the blends: BL, CL, FL, GL, PL, SL, BR, CR, DR, FR, GR, PR, TR, SC, SK, SM, SN, SP, ST, SW, TW.
- *Consonant* Diagraphs: diagraphs are two letters that make one sound. The diagraphs are TH, CH, SH, WH.
- *Complex Consonants:* blends that include three consonants, two consonants that sounds like a single letter, and consonant and vowel clusters. The complex consonants are QU, TCH.
  - CK Rule makes the /k/ sound (example: so**ck**)

Recommended (Age Appropriate) Reading Chunks

- Verses 1–7
- Verses 8–14
- Verses 15–22

Gospel Principle Review/Activity

- What is the Millennium?
- *Activity:* The Lord talks about His house being in the "top of the mountains." How do temples look like mountains?
  - Draw a picture of a mountain
  - On another sheet of paper, draw a picture of a temple. Then lay one on top of the other. Are they similar?

Word Patterns

_ock

Lesson 34: words made with –ock word pattern.
Use alphabet letters to create words.

Nephi 12

1 The word that Isaiah, the son of Amoz, saw concerning Judah and Jerusalem:

2 And it shall come to pass in the last days, when the mountain of the Lord's house shall be established in the top of the mountains, and shall be exalted above the hills, and all nations shall flow unto it.

3 And many people shall go and say, Come ye, and let us go up to the mountain of the Lord, to the house of the God of Jacob; and he will teach us of his ways, and we will walk in his paths; for out of Zion shall go forth the law, and the word of the Lord from Jerusalem.

4 And he shall judge among the nations, and shall rebuke many people: and they shall beat their swords into plow-shares, and their spears into pruning-hooks—nation shall not lift up sword against nation, neither shall they learn war any more.

5 O house of Jacob, come ye and let us walk in the light of the Lord; yea, come, for ye have all gone astray, every one to his wicked ways.

6 Therefore, O Lord, thou hast forsaken thy people, the house of Jacob, because they be replenished from the east, and hearken unto soothsayers like the Philistines, and they please themselves in the children of strangers.

7 Their land also is full of silver and gold, neither is there any end of their treasures; their land is also full of horses, neither is there any end of their chariots.

8 Their land is also full of idols; they worship the work of their own hands, that which their own fingers have made.

9 And the mean man boweth not down, and the great man humbleth himself not, therefore, forgive him not.

10 O ye wicked ones, enter into the rock, and hide thee in the dust, for the fear of the Lord and the glory of his majesty shall smite thee.

11 And it shall come to pass that the lofty looks of man shall be humbled, and the haughtiness of men shall be bowed down, and the Lord alone shall be exalted in that day.

12 For the day of the Lord of Hosts soon cometh upon all nations, yea, upon every one; yea, upon the proud and lofty, and upon every one who is lifted up, and he shall be brought low.

13 Yea, and the day of the Lord shall come upon all the cedars of Lebanon, for they are high and lifted up; and upon all the oaks of Bashan;

14 And upon all the high mountains, and upon all the hills, and upon all the nations which are lifted up, and upon every people;

15 And upon every high tower, and upon every fenced wall;

16 And upon all the ships of the sea, and upon all the ships of Tarshish, and upon all pleasant pictures.

Date _____
☐ Completed

Date _____
☐ Completed

17 And the loftiness of man shall be bowed down, and the haughtiness of men shall be made low; and the Lord alone shall be exalted in that day.

18 And the idols he shall utterly abolish.

19 And they shall go into the holes of the rocks, and into the caves of the earth, for the fear of the Lord shall come upon them and the glory of his majesty shall smite them, when he ariseth to shake terribly the earth.

20 In that day a man shall cast his idols of silver, and his idols of gold, which he hath made for himself to worship, to the moles and to the bats;

21 To go into the clefts of the rocks, and into the tops of the ragged rocks, for the fear of the Lord shall come upon them and the majesty of his glory shall smite them, when he ariseth to shake terribly the earth.

22 Cease ye from man, whose breath is in his nostrils; for wherein is he to be accounted of?

Notes

Date _____

☐ Completed

2 Nephi

Chapter 13

Sight (Memorization) Words

me

Word Pattern

Pattern	-ell
Pattern words in scriptures	**well, smell**
Location in chapter	Verse 41
Other words made from this patterns not found in chapter	bell, dell, dwell, fell, hell, Nell, sell, tell, yell, spell, swell, shell

Phonics Application

- *Words that end with vowels:* when a word ends with a vowel and it is the only vowel in the word, the vowel is usually a LONG vowel, or a vowel that says its name (example: me).
- *Short vowel sounds:* the sound of the letter phonetically (versus the long sound or name of the letter).
  - The short sound of E (example: b**e**d)
- *Consonant-Vowel-Blend and Blend-Vowel-Blend:* these patterns are the merging together of sounds to make words. A blend is the combination of two (or more) consonants together. These are the blends: BL, CL, FL, GL, PL, SL, BR, CR, DR, FR, GR, PR, TR, SC, SK, SM, SN, SP, ST, SW, TW.
- *Consonant Diagraphs:* diagraphs are two letters that make one sound. The diagraphs are TH, CH, SH, WH.
- *Complex Consonants:* blends that include three consonants, two consonants that sounds like a single letter, and consonant and vowel clusters. The complex consonants are QU, TCH, CK.
- *Doublet:* a special type of across-syllable pattern in which the two consonants are the same.
  - LL (example: ba**ll**)

Recommended (Age Appropriate) Reading Chunks

- Verses 1–8
- Verses 9–15
- Verses 16–26

Gospel Principle Review/Activity

- Why were women in this chapter wearing all those ornaments?
- *Activity:* The Lord teaches us that "the show of their countenance doth witness against them." This means that you can tell what people are feeling by looking at their faces. Take a piece of paper the next time you go to the store. Look at people's faces and write down which emotion you think they are feeling. Do you think people can tell what you are feeling?

Word Patterns

ell

Lesson 35: words made with –ell word pattern.
Use alphabet letters to create words.

2 Nephi 13

1 For behold, the Lord, the Lord of Hosts, doth take away from Jerusalem, and from Judah, the stay and the staff, the whole staff of bread, and the whole stay of water—

2 The mighty man, and the man of war, the judge, and the prophet, and the prudent, and the ancient;

3 The captain of fifty, and the honorable man, and the counselor, and the cunning artificer, and the eloquent orator.

4 And I will give children unto them to be their princes, and babes shall rule over them.

5 And the people shall be oppressed, every one by another, and every one by his neighbor; the child shall behave himself proudly against the ancient, and the base against the honorable.

6 When a man shall take hold of his brother of the house of his father, and shall say: Thou hast clothing, be thou our ruler, and let not this ruin come under thy hand—

7 In that day shall he swear, saying: I will not be a healer; for in my house there is neither bread nor clothing; make me not a ruler of the people.

8 For Jerusalem is ruined, and Judah is fallen, because their tongues and their doings have been against the Lord, to provoke the eyes of his glory.

9 The show of their countenance doth witness against them, and doth declare their sin to be even as Sodom, and they cannot hide it. Wo unto their souls, for they have rewarded evil unto themselves!

10 Say unto the righteous that it is well with them; for they shall eat the fruit of their doings.

11 Wo unto the wicked, for they shall perish; for the reward of their hands shall be upon them!

12 And my people, children are their oppressors, and women rule over them. O my people, they who lead thee cause thee to err and destroy the way of thy paths.

13 The Lord standeth up to plead, and standeth to judge the people.

14 The Lord will enter into judgment with the ancients of his people and the princes thereof; for ye have eaten up the vineyard and the spoil of the poor in your houses.

15 What mean ye? Ye beat my people to pieces, and grind the faces of the poor, saith the Lord God of Hosts.

16 Moreover, the Lord saith: Because the daughters of Zion are haughty, and walk with stretched–forth necks and wanton eyes, walking and mincing as they go, and making a tinkling with their feet—

17 Therefore the Lord will smite with a scab the crown of the head of the daughters of Zion, and the Lord will discover their secret parts.

18 In that day the Lord will take away the bravery of their tinkling ornaments, and cauls, and round tires like the moon;

19 The chains and the bracelets, and the mufflers;

20 The bonnets, and the ornaments of the legs, and the headbands, and the tablets, and the ear-rings;

21 The rings, and nose jewels;

22 The changeable suits of apparel, and the mantles, and the wimples, and the crisping–pins;

23 The glasses, and the fine linen, and hoods, and the veils.

24 And it shall come to pass, instead of sweet smell there shall be stink; and instead of a girdle, a rent; and instead of well set hair, baldness; and instead of a stomacher, a girding of sackcloth; burning instead of beauty.

25 Thy men shall fall by the sword and thy mighty in the war.

26 And her gates shall lament and mourn; and she shall be desolate, and shall sit upon the ground.

Notes

Date _____

☐ Completed

2 Nephi

Chapter 14

Sight (Memorization) Words

our

(Note: the -ou pattern is related to the abstract vowels—abnormal sounds explained in Alma 8.)

Word Pattern

Pattern	-all
Pattern words in scriptures	**shall**
Location in chapter	Verse 10
Exceptions to the rule	all, ball, call, doll, fall, gall, hall, mall, tall, wall stall (2 Nephi 2)
Other words made from this patterns not found in chapter	(none listed)

Phonics Application

- *Short vowel sounds:* the sound of the letter phonetically (versus the long sound or name of the letter).
  - The short sound of A (example: **a**pple)
- *Consonant-Vowel-Blend and Blend-Vowel-Blend:* these patterns are the merging together of sounds to make words. A blend is the combination of two (or more) consonants together. These are the blends: BL, CL, FL, GL, PL, SL, BR, CR, DR, FR, GR, PR, TR, SC, SK, SM, SN, SP, ST, SW, TW.
- *Consonant Diagraphs:* diagraphs are two letters that make one sound. The diagraphs are TH, CH, SH, WH.
- *Complex Consonants:* blends that include three consonants, two consonants that sounds like a single letter, and consonant and vowel clusters. The Complex Consonants are QU, TCH, CK.
- *Doublet:* a special type of across-syllable pattern in which the two consonants are the same.
  - LL (example: ba**ll**)

Recommended (Age Appropriate) Reading Chunks

- Verses 1–6

Gospel Principle Review/Activity

- Why do you think the Lord lets the saints be persecuted?
- *Activity:* Isaiah tells us in the last days that men and women will say, "We will eat our own bread, and wear our own apparel." What is the difference between buying and making your own bread?
  - Bake your own loaf of bread. Is it more special to you than store bought bread? Why? What is the Lord trying to teach us?

Word Patterns

all
___

Lesson 36: words made with –all word pattern.
Use alphabet letters to create words.

2 Nephi 14

1 And in that day, seven women shall take hold of one man, saying: We will eat our own bread, and wear our own apparel; only let us be called by thy name to take away our reproach.

2 In that day shall the branch of the Lord be beautiful and glorious; the fruit of the earth excellent and comely to them that are escaped of Israel.

3 And it shall come to pass, they that are left in Zion and remain in Jerusalem shall be called holy, every one that is written among the living in Jerusalem—

4 When the Lord shall have washed away the filth of the daughters of Zion, and shall have purged the blood of Jerusalem from the midst thereof by the spirit of judgment and by the spirit of burning.

5 And the Lord will create upon every dwelling–place of mount Zion, and upon her assemblies, a cloud and smoke by day and the shining of a flaming fire by night; for upon all the glory of Zion shall be a defence.

6 And there shall be a tabernacle for a shadow in the daytime from the heat, and for a place of refuge, and a covert from storm and from rain.

2 Nephi

Chapter 15

Sight (Memorization) Words

Word Pattern

Pattern	-ong
Pattern words in scriptures	**strong**
Location in chapter	Verses 1, 11–22
Other words made from this patterns not found in chapter	gong, long, pong

Phonics Application

- *Short vowel sounds:* the sound of the letter phonetically (versus the long sound or name of the letter).
  - The short sound of O (example: h**o**p)
- *Consonant-Vowel-Blend and Blend-Vowel-Blend:* these patterns are the merging together of sounds to make words. A blend is the combination of two (or more) consonants together. These are the blends: BL, CL, FL, GL, PL, SL, BR, CR, DR, FR, GR, PR, TR, SC, SK, SM, SN, SP, ST, SW, TW.
- *Consonant Diagraphs:* diagraphs are two letters that make one sound. The diagraphs are TH, CH, SH, WH.
- *Complex Consonants:* blends that include three consonants, two consonants that sounds like a single letter, and consonant and vowel clusters. The complex consonants are QU, TCH, CK.

Recommended (Age Appropriate) Reading Chunks

- Verses 1–7
- Verses 8–14
- Verses 15–23
- Verses 24–30

Gospel Principle Review/Activity

- What item represented the "word of God"?
- *Activity:* The Lord speaks of lifting up an "ensign to the nations." An ensign is like a flag or a banner.
  - Make a family banner.
  - What would you write on it?

Word Patterns

ong

Lesson 37: words made with –ong word pattern.
Use alphabet letters to create words.

2 Nephi 15

1 And then will I sing to my well-beloved a song of my beloved, touching his vineyard. My well-beloved hath a vineyard in a very fruitful hill.

2 And he fenced it, and gathered out the stones thereof, and planted it with the choicest vine, and built a tower in the midst of it, and also made a wine–press therein; and he looked that it should bring forth grapes, and it brought forth wild grapes.

3 And now, O inhabitants of Jerusalem, and men of Judah, judge, I pray you, betwixt me and my vineyard.

4 What could have been done more to my vineyard that I have not done in it? Wherefore, when I looked that it should bring forth grapes it brought forth wild grapes.

5 And now go to; I will tell you what I will do to my vineyard—I will take away the hedge thereof, and it shall be eaten up; and I will break down the wall thereof, and it shall be trodden down;

6 And I will lay it waste; it shall not be pruned nor digged; but there shall come up briers and thorns; I will also command the clouds that they rain no rain upon it.

7 For the vineyard of the Lord of Hosts is the house of Israel, and the men of Judah his pleasant plant; and he looked for judgment, and behold, oppression; for righteousness, but behold, a cry.

8 Wo unto them that join house to house, till there can be no place, that they may be placed alone in the midst of the earth!

9 In mine ears, said the Lord of Hosts, of a truth many houses shall be desolate, and great and fair cities without inhabitant.

10 Yea, ten acres of vineyard shall yield one bath, and the seed of a homer shall yield an ephah.

11 Wo unto them that rise up early in the morning, that they may follow strong drink, that continue until night, and wine inflame them!

12 And the harp, and the viol, the tabret, and pipe, and wine are in their feasts; but they regard not the work of the Lord, neither consider the operation of his hands.

13 Therefore, my people are gone into captivity, because they have no knowledge; and their honorable men are famished, and their multitude dried up with thirst.

14 Therefore, hell hath enlarged herself, and opened her mouth without measure; and their glory, and their multitude, and their pomp, and he that rejoiceth, shall descend into it.

15 And the mean man shall be brought down, and the mighty man shall be humbled, and the eyes of the lofty shall be humbled.

16 But the Lord of Hosts shall be exalted in judgment, and God that is holy shall be sanctified in righteousness.

17 Then shall the lambs feed after their manner, and the waste places of the fat ones shall strangers eat.

18 Wo unto them that draw iniquity with cords of vanity, and sin as it were with a cart rope;

19 That say: Let him make speed, hasten his work, that we may see it; and let the counsel of the Holy One of Israel draw nigh and come, that we may know it.

20 Wo unto them that call evil good, and good evil, that put darkness for light, and light for darkness, that put bitter for sweet, and sweet for bitter!

21 Wo unto the wise in their own eyes and prudent in their own sight!

22 Wo unto the mighty to drink wine, and men of strength to mingle strong drink;

23 Who justify the wicked for reward, and take away the righteousness of the righteous from him!

_____

24 Therefore, as the fire devoureth the stubble, and the flame consumeth the chaff, their root shall be rottenness, and their blossoms shall go up as dust; because they have cast away the law of the Lord of Hosts, and despised the word of the Holy One of Israel.

25 Therefore, is the anger of the Lord kindled against his people, and he hath stretched forth his hand against them, and hath smitten them; and the hills did tremble, and their carcasses were torn in the midst of the streets. For all this his anger is not turned away, but his hand is stretched out still.

26 And he will lift up an ensign to the nations from far, and will hiss unto them from the end of the earth; and behold, they shall come with speed swiftly; none shall be weary nor stumble among them.

27 None shall slumber nor sleep; neither shall the girdle of their loins be loosed, nor the latchet of their shoes be broken;

28 Whose arrows shall be sharp, and all their bows bent, and their horses' hoofs shall be counted like flint, and their wheels like a whirlwind, their roaring like a lion.

29 They shall roar like young lions; yea, they shall roar, and lay hold of the prey, and shall carry away safe, and none shall deliver.

30 And in that day they shall roar against them like the roaring of the sea; and if they look unto the land, behold, darkness and sorrow, and the light is darkened in the heavens thereof.

2 Nephi

Chapter 16—Review

Sight (Memorization) Words

says	also	gold	me	our	evil

Word Pattern

Pattern	-ond	-ill	-ock	-ell	-all	-ong
Pattern words reviewed	bond	will	rock	well	shall	song, strong

Phonics Application

- *Short vowel sounds:* the sound of the letter phonetically (versus the long sound or name of the letter).
  - The short sound of A (example: **a**pple)
  - The short sound of I (example: h**i**t)
  - The short sound of O (example: h**o**p)
- *Consonant-Vowel-Blend and Blend-Vowel-Blend:* these patterns are the merging together of sounds to make words. A blend is the combination of two (or more) consonants together. These are the blends: BL, CL, FL, GL, PL, SL, BR, CR, DR, FR, GR, PR, TR, SC, SK, SM, SN, SP, ST, SW, TW.
- *Consonant Diagraphs:* diagraphs are two letters that make one sound. The diagraphs are TH, CH, SH, WH.
- *Complex Consonants:* blends that include three consonants, two consonants that sounds like a single letter, and consonant and vowel clusters. The complex consonants are QU, TCH, CK.
- *Doublet:* a special type of across-syllable pattern in which the two consonants are the same.
  - LL (example: ba**ll**)

Recommended (Age Appropriate) Reading Chunks

- Verses 1-7
- Verses 8-13

Gospel Principle Review/Activity

- Why do the wicked take the truth to be hard?
- Who answered when the Lord asked, "Whom shall I send?"
- *Activity:* It is hard to envision some of the things that Isaiah sees. He sees a seraphim and talks about what it would look like in verse 2. Take a sheet of paper and draw what a seraphim looks like from Isaiah's description.

Word Patterns—Review

Lesson 38 Review: Find the words in the word box in the word search.

Word Box

pond	shell
hill	ball
rock	long

```
J  C  X  K  F  Z  T  W  U  C
H  R  C  D  H  E  P  O  K  M
T  O  L  C  N  G  E  L  Y  E
R  H  O  O  H  O  G  L  Z  J
G  L  Q  D  N  B  P  L  B  X
L  L  E  H  S  G  H  I  Z  I
B  A  L  L  C  Q  F  H  Y  L
M  J  N  X  O  Y  S  V  V  O
D  F  W  W  Y  U  M  H  I  Z
F  M  N  D  Q  M  V  J  M  T
```

2 Nephi 16

1 In the year that king Uzziah died, I saw also the Lord sitting upon a throne, high and lifted up, and his train filled the temple.

2 Above it stood the seraphim; each one had six wings; with twain he covered his face, and with twain he covered his feet, and with twain he did fly.

3 And one cried unto another, and said: Holy, holy, holy, is the Lord of Hosts; the whole earth is full of his glory.

4 And the posts of the door moved at the voice of him that cried, and the house was filled with smoke.

5 Then said I: Wo is unto me! for I am undone; because I am a man of unclean lips; and I dwell in the midst of a people of unclean lips; for mine eyes have seen the King, the Lord of Hosts.

6 Then flew one of the seraphim unto me, having a live coal in his hand, which he had taken with the tongs from off the altar;

7 And he laid it upon my mouth, and said: Lo, this has touched thy lips; and thine iniquity is taken away, and thy sin purged.

8 Also I heard the voice of the Lord, saying: Whom shall I send, and who will go for us? Then I said: Here am I; send me.

9 And he said: Go and tell this people—Hear ye indeed, but they understood not; and see ye indeed, but they perceived not.

10 Make the heart of this people fat, and make their ears heavy, and shut their eyes—lest they see with their eyes, and hear with their ears, and understand with their heart, and be converted and be healed.

11 Then said I: Lord, how long? And he said: Until the cities be wasted without inhabitant, and the houses without man, and the land be utterly desolate;

12 And the Lord have removed men far away, for there shall be a great forsaking in the midst of the land.

13 But yet there shall be a tenth, and they shall return, and shall be eaten, as a teil–tree, and as an oak whose substance is in them when they cast their leaves; so the holy seed shall be the substance thereof.

Date _____
☐ Completed

Date _____
☐ Completed

2 Nephi

Chapter 17

Sight (Memorization) Words

son

Word Pattern

Pattern	-ind
Pattern words in scriptures	**wind**
Location in chapter	Verse 2
Exceptions to the rule	bind, find, kind, mind, rind, wind (long I)
Other words made from this patterns not found in chapter	(none listed)

Phonics Application

- *Short vowel sounds:* the sound of the letter phonetically (versus the long sound or name of the letter).
  - The short sound of A (example: **a**pple)
- *Consonant-Vowel-Blend and Blend-Vowel-Blend:* these patterns are the merging together of sounds to make words. A blend is the combination of two (or more) consonants together. These are the blends: BL, CL, FL, GL, PL, SL, BR, CR, DR, FR, GR, PR, TR, SC, SK, SM, SN, SP, ST, SW, TW.
- *Consonant Diagraphs:* diagraphs are two letters that make one sound. The diagraphs are TH, CH, SH, WH.
- *Complex Consonants:* blends that include three consonants, two consonants that sounds like a single letter, and consonant and vowel clusters. The complex consonants are QU, TCH, CK.

Recommended (Age Appropriate) Reading Chunks

- Verses 1–7
- Verses 8–16
- Verses 17–25

Gospel Principle Review/Activity

- Why did Ephraim and Syria go to war against Judah? (Refer to 2 Kings 15.)
- *Activity:* Who is going to be born of a virgin? Who is the virgin? Did this happen? Read Luke 2 to see if this prophecy was fulfilled.

Word Patterns

ind

Lesson 39: words made with –ind word pattern.
Use alphabet letters to create words.

Note: there are two types of sounds this pattern makes, the short I and the long I.

Place the correct word in the correct category.

Short I

Long I

2 Nephi 17

1 And it came to pass in the days of Ahaz the son of Jotham, the son of Uzziah, king of Judah, that Rezin, king of Syria, and Pekah the son of Remaliah, king of Israel, went up toward Jerusalem to war against it, but could not prevail against it.

2 And it was told the house of David, saying: Syria is confederate with Ephraim. And his heart was moved, and the heart of his people, as the trees of the wood are moved with the wind.

3 Then said the Lord unto Isaiah: Go forth now to meet Ahaz, thou and Shearjashub thy son, at the end of the conduit of the upper pool in the highway of the fuller's field;

4 And say unto him: Take heed, and be quiet; fear not, neither be faint-hearted for the two tails of these smoking firebrands, for the fierce anger of Rezin with Syria, and of the son of Remaliah.

5 Because Syria, Ephraim, and the son of Remaliah, have taken evil counsel against thee, saying:

6 Let us go up against Judah and vex it, and let us make a breach therein for us, and set a king in the midst of it, yea, the son of Tabeal.

7 Thus saith the Lord God: It shall not stand, neither shall it come to pass.

8 For the head of Syria is Damascus, and the head of Damascus, Rezin; and within three score and five years shall Ephraim be broken that it be not a people.

9 And the head of Ephraim is Samaria, and the head of Samaria is Remaliah's son. If ye will not believe surely ye shall not be established.

10 Moreover, the Lord spake again unto Ahaz, saying:

11 Ask thee a sign of the Lord thy God; ask it either in the depths, or in the heights above.

12 But Ahaz said: I will not ask, neither will I tempt the Lord.

13 And he said: Hear ye now, O house of David; is it a small thing for you to weary men, but will ye weary my God also?

14 Therefore, the Lord himself shall give you a sign—Behold, a virgin shall conceive, and shall bear a son, and shall call his name Immanuel.

15 Butter and honey shall he eat, that he may know to refuse the evil and to choose the good.

16 For before the child shall know to refuse the evil and choose the good, the land that thou abhorrest shall be forsaken of both her kings.

17 The Lord shall bring upon thee, and upon thy people, and upon thy father's house, days that have not come from the day that Ephraim departed from Judah, the king of Assyria.

18 And it shall come to pass in that day that the Lord shall hiss for the fly that is in the uttermost part of Egypt, and for the bee that is in the land of Assyria.

19 And they shall come, and shall rest all of them in the desolate valleys, and in the holes of the rocks, and upon all thorns, and upon all bushes.

20 In the same day shall the Lord shave with a razor that is hired, by them beyond the river, by the king of Assyria, the head, and the hair of the feet; and it shall also consume the beard.

21 And it shall come to pass in that day, a man shall nourish a young cow and two sheep;

22 And it shall come to pass, for the abundance of milk they shall give he shall eat butter; for butter and honey shall every one eat that is left in the land.

23 And it shall come to pass in that day, every place shall be, where there were a thousand vines at a thousand silverlings, which shall be for briers and thorns.

24 With arrows and with bows shall men come thither, because all the land shall become briers and thorns.

25 And all hills that shall be digged with the mattock, there shall not come thither the fear of briers and thorns; but it shall be for the sending forth of oxen, and the treading of lesser cattle.

Date _____

☐ Completed

2 Nephi

Chapter 18

Sight (Memorization) Words

Also stalk, talk

Word Pattern

Pattern	-eck
Pattern words in scriptures	**neck**
Location in chapter	Verse 8
Exceptions to the rule	wreck, trek
Other words made from this patterns not found in chapter	deck, heck, peck, speck

Phonics Application

- *Short vowel sounds:* the sound of the letter phonetically (versus the long sound or name of the letter).
  - The short sound of E (example: bed)
- *Consonant-Vowel-Blend and Blend-Vowel-Blend:* these patterns are the merging together of sounds to make words. A blend is the combination of two (or more) consonants together. These are the blends: BL, CL, FL, GL, PL, SL, BR, CR, DR, FR, GR, PR, TR, SC, SK, SM, SN, SP, ST, SW, TW.
- *Consonant Diagraphs:* diagraphs are two letters that make one sound. The diagraphs are TH, CH, SH, WH.
- *Complex Consonants:* blends that include three consonants, two consonants that sounds like a single letter, and consonant and vowel clusters. The complex consonants are QU, TCH, CK.

Recommended (Age Appropriate) Reading Chunks

- Verses 1–8
- Verses 9–16
- Verses 17–22

Gospel Principle Review/Activity

- Why is it better to seek the Lord and not "peeping wizards"?
- Why is Christ a "stone of stumbling" or a "rock of offense"?
- *Activity:* How can we "seek the Lord"? Play a game of hide-and-go-seek. (One person counts while others hide. After counting, the person goes to find those who are hiding. The last person found wins).
  - How is this game similar to seeking the Lord?

Word Patterns

_eck

Lesson 40: words made with –eck word pattern.
Use alphabet letters to create words.

2 Nephi 18

1 Moreover, the word of the Lord said unto me: Take thee a great roll, and write in it with a man's pen, concerning Maher-shalal-hash-baz.
2 And I took unto me faithful witnesses to record, Uriah the priest, and Zechariah the son of Jeberechiah.
3 And I went unto the prophetess; and she conceived and bare a son. Then said the Lord to me: Call his name, Maher-shalal-hash-baz.
4 For behold, the child shall not have knowledge to cry, My father, and my mother, before the riches of Damascus and the spoil of Samaria shall be taken away before the king of Assyria.
5 The Lord spake also unto me again, saying:
6 Forasmuch as this people refuseth the waters of Shiloah that go softly, and rejoice in Rezin and Remaliah's son;
7 Now therefore, behold, the Lord bringeth up upon them the waters of the river, strong and many, even the king of Assyria and all his glory; and he shall come up over all his channels, and go over all his banks.
8 And he shall pass through Judah; he shall overflow and go over, he shall reach even to the neck; and the stretching out of his wings shall fill the breadth of thy land, O Immanuel.

9 Associate yourselves, O ye people, and ye shall be broken in pieces; and give ear all ye of far countries; gird yourselves, and ye shall be broken in pieces; gird yourselves, and ye shall be broken in pieces.
10 Take counsel together, and it shall come to naught; speak the word, and it shall not stand; for God is with us.
11 For the Lord spake thus to me with a strong hand, and instructed me that I should not walk in the way of this people, saying:
12 Say ye not, A confederacy, to all to whom this people shall say, A confederacy; neither fear ye their fear, nor be afraid.
13 Sanctify the Lord of Hosts himself, and let him be your fear, and let him be your dread.
14 And he shall be for a sanctuary; but for a stone of stumbling, and for a rock of offense to both the houses of Israel, for a gin and a snare to the inhabitants of Jerusalem.
15 And many among them shall stumble and fall, and be broken, and be snared, and be taken.
16 Bind up the testimony, seal the law among my disciples.

17 And I will wait upon the Lord, that hideth his face from the house of Jacob, and I will look for him.
18 Behold, I and the children whom the Lord hath given me are for signs and for wonders in Israel from the Lord of Hosts, which dwelleth in Mount Zion.

Date _____
☐ Completed

Date _____
☐ Completed

19 And when they shall say unto you: Seek unto them that have familiar spirits, and unto wizards that peep and mutter—should not a people seek unto their God for the living to hear from the dead?

20 To the law and to the testimony; and if they speak not according to this word, it is because there is no light in them.

21 And they shall pass through it hardly bestead and hungry; and it shall come to pass that when they shall be hungry, they shall fret themselves, and curse their king and their God, and look upward.

22 And they shall look unto the earth and behold trouble, and darkness, dimness of anguish, and shall be driven to darkness.

2 Nephi

Chapter 19

Sight (Memorization) Words

thee

(Note: the -ee pattern is related to the double vowels explained in Mosiah 4:6. The TH sounds are explained in 1 Nephi 3.)

Word Pattern

Pattern	-end
Pattern words in scriptures	**end**
Location in chapter	Verse 7
Exceptions to the rule	friend
Other words made from this patterns not found in chapter	bend, fend, lend, mend, send, tend, vend, blend, trend, spend

Phonics Application

- *Words that end with vowels:* when a word ends with a vowel and it is the only vowel in the word, the vowel is usually a LONG vowel, or a vowel that says its name (example: n**o**).
- *Short vowel sounds:* the sound of the letter phonetically (versus the long sound or name of the letter).
  - The short sound of E (example: b**e**d)
- *Consonant-Vowel-Blend and Blend-Vowel-Blend:* these patterns are the merging together of sounds to make words. A blend is the combination of two (or more) consonants together. These are the blends: BL, CL, FL, GL, PL, SL, BR, CR, DR, FR, GR, PR, TR, SC, SK, SM, SN, SP, ST, SW, TW.
- *Consonant Diagraphs:* diagraphs are two letters that make one sound. The diagraphs are TH, CH, SH, WH.
- *Complex Consonants:* blends that include three consonants, two consonants that sounds like a single letter, and consonant and vowel clusters. The complex consonants are QU, TCH, CK.

Recommended (Age Appropriate) Reading Chunks

- Verses 1–7
- Verses 8–16
- Verses 17–21

Gospel Principle Review/Activity

- What light do the people in darkness see?
- *Activity:* In verse 6, there are phrases that are used to describe Christ. These phrases are sometimes called nicknames. People usually earn nicknames because of something they do or because of qualities they have.
  - Can you think of another phrase or nickname to describe Christ?
  - What is a nickname you want to be known by?

Word Patterns

end

Lesson 41: words made with –end word pattern.
Use alphabet letters to create words.

181

2 Nephi 19

1 Nevertheless, the dimness shall not be such as was in her vexation, when at first he lightly afflicted the land of Zebulun, and the land of Naphtali, and afterwards did more grievously afflict by the way of the Red Sea beyond Jordan in Galilee of the nations.

2 The people that walked in darkness have seen a great light; they that dwell in the land of the shadow of death, upon them hath the light shined.

3 Thou hast multiplied the nation, and increased the joy—they joy before thee according to the joy in harvest, and as men rejoice when they divide the spoil.

4 For thou hast broken the yoke of his burden, and the staff of his shoulder, the rod of his oppressor.

5 For every battle of the warrior is with confused noise, and garments rolled in blood; but this shall be with burning and fuel of fire.

6 For unto us a child is born, unto us a son is given; and the government shall be upon his shoulder; and his name shall be called, Wonderful, Counselor, The Mighty God, The Everlasting Father, The Prince of Peace.

7 Of the increase of government and peace there is no end, upon the throne of David, and upon his kingdom to order it, and to establish it with judgment and with justice from henceforth, even forever. The zeal of the Lord of Hosts will perform this.

Date _____
☐ Completed

8 The Lord sent his word unto Jacob and it hath lighted upon Israel.

9 And all the people shall know, even Ephraim and the inhabitants of Samaria, that say in the pride and stoutness of heart:

10 The bricks are fallen down, but we will build with hewn stones; the sycamores are cut down, but we will change them into cedars.

11 Therefore the Lord shall set up the adversaries of Rezin against him, and join his enemies together;

12 The Syrians before and the Philistines behind; and they shall devour Israel with open mouth. For all this his anger is not turned away, but his hand is stretched out still.

13 For the people turneth not unto him that smiteth them, neither do they seek the Lord of Hosts.

14 Therefore will the Lord cut off from Israel head and tail, branch and rush in one day.

15 The ancient, he is the head; and the prophet that teacheth lies, he is the tail.

16 For the leaders of this people cause them to err; and they that are led of them are destroyed.

Date _____
☐ Completed

17 Therefore the Lord shall have no joy in their young men, neither shall have mercy on their fatherless and widows; for every one of them is a hypocrite and an evildoer, and every mouth speaketh folly. For all this his anger is not turned away, but his hand is stretched out still.

18 For wickedness burneth as the fire; it shall devour the briers and thorns, and shall kindle in the thickets of the forests, and they shall mount up like the lifting up of smoke.

19 Through the wrath of the Lord of Hosts is the land darkened, and the people shall be as the fuel of the fire; no man shall spare his brother.

20 And he shall snatch on the right hand and be hungry; and he shall eat on the left hand and they shall not be satisfied; they shall eat every man the flesh of his own arm—

21 Manasseh, Ephraim; and Ephraim, Manasseh; they together shall be against Judah. For all this his anger is not turned away, but his hand is stretched out still.

Notes

Date _____
☐ Completed

2 Nephi

Chapter 20

Sight (Memorization) Words

> **out**

(Note: the -ou pattern is related to the abstract vowels—abnormal sounds explained in Alma 8.)

Word Pattern

Pattern	-elp
Pattern words in scriptures	**help**
Location in chapter	Verse 3
Other words made from this patterns not found in chapter	kelp, yelp

Phonics Application

- *Short vowel sounds:* the sound of the letter phonetically (versus the long sound or name of the letter).
  - The short sound of E (example: b**e**d)
- *Consonant-Vowel-Blend and Blend-Vowel-Blend:* these patterns are the merging together of sounds to make words. A blend is the combination of two (or more) consonants together. These are the blends: BL, CL, FL, GL, PL, SL, BR, CR, DR, FR, GR, PR, TR, SC, SK, SM, SN, SP, ST, SW, TW.
- *Consonant Diagraphs:* diagraphs are two letters that make one sound. The diagraphs are TH, CH, SH, WH.
- *Complex Consonants:* blends that include three consonants, two consonants that sounds like a single letter, and consonant and vowel clusters. The complex consonants are QU, TCH, CK.

Recommended (Age Appropriate) Reading Chunks

- Verses 1–8
- Verses 9–14
- Verses 15–23
- Verses 24–34

Gospel Principle Review/Activity

- How does the destruction of Assyria relate to the destruction before the Second Coming of Christ?
- *Activity:* This chapter often mentions a "rod." What is a rod? Introduce your student to the Bible Dictionary (not included in this manual). Look up the word *rod*. There are many definitions. Write down the different definitions, and then circle the definition that this chapter uses.

  - Definition 1: _____
  - Definition 2: _____
  - Definition 3: _____
  - Definition 4: _____
  - Definition 5: _____

Word Patterns

elp

Lesson 42: words made with –elp word pattern.
Use alphabet letters to create words.

2 Nephi 20

1 Wo unto them that decree unrighteous decrees, and that write grievousness which they have prescribed;

2 To turn away the needy from judgment, and to take away the right from the poor of my people, that widows may be their prey, and that they may rob the fatherless!

3 And what will ye do in the day of visitation, and in the desolation which shall come from far? to whom will ye flee for help? and where will ye leave your glory?

4 Without me they shall bow down under the prisoners, and they shall fall under the slain. For all this his anger is not turned away, but his hand is stretched out still.

5 O Assyrian, the rod of mine anger, and the staff in their hand is their indignation.

6 I will send him against a hypocritical nation, and against the people of my wrath will I give him a charge to take the spoil, and to take the prey, and to tread them down like the mire of the streets.

7 Howbeit he meaneth not so, neither doth his heart think so; but in his heart it is to destroy and cut off nations not a few.

8 For he saith: Are not my princes altogether kings?

Date _____
☐ Completed

9 Is not Calno as Carchemish? Is not Hamath as Arpad? Is not Samaria as Damascus?

10 As my hand hath founded the kingdoms of the idols, and whose graven images did excel them of Jerusalem and of Samaria;

11 Shall I not, as I have done unto Samaria and her idols, so do to Jerusalem and to her idols?

12 Wherefore it shall come to pass that when the Lord hath performed his whole work upon Mount Zion and upon Jerusalem, I will punish the fruit of the stout heart of the king of Assyria, and the glory of his high looks.

13 For he saith: By the strength of my hand and by my wisdom I have done these things; for I am prudent; and I have moved the borders of the people, and have robbed their treasures, and I have put down the inhabitants like a valiant man;

14 And my hand hath found as a nest the riches of the people; and as one gathereth eggs that are left have I gathered all the earth; and there was none that moved the wing, or opened the mouth, or peeped.

Date _____
☐ Completed

15 Shall the ax boast itself against him that heweth therewith? Shall the saw magnify itself against him that shaketh it? As if the rod should shake itself against them that lift it up, or as if the staff should lift up itself as if it were no wood!

16 Therefore shall the Lord, the Lord of Hosts, send among his fat ones, leanness; and under his glory he shall kindle a burning like the burning of a fire.
17 And the light of Israel shall be for a fire, and his Holy One for a flame, and shall burn and shall devour his thorns and his briers in one day;
18 And shall consume the glory of his forest, and of his fruitful field, both soul and body; and they shall be as when a standard–bearer fainteth.
19 And the rest of the trees of his forest shall be few, that a child may write them.
20 And it shall come to pass in that day, that the remnant of Israel, and such as are escaped of the house of Jacob, shall no more again stay upon him that smote them, but shall stay upon the Lord, the Holy One of Israel, in truth.
21 The remnant shall return, yea, even the remnant of Jacob, unto the mighty God.
22 For though thy people Israel be as the sand of the sea, yet a remnant of them shall return; the consumption decreed shall overflow with righteousness.
23 For the Lord God of Hosts shall make a consumption, even determined in all the land.

24 Therefore, thus saith the Lord God of Hosts: O my people that dwellest in Zion, be not afraid of the Assyrian; he shall smite thee with a rod, and shall lift up his staff against thee, after the manner of Egypt.
25 For yet a very little while, and the indignation shall cease, and mine anger in their destruction.
26 And the Lord of Hosts shall stir up a scourge for him according to the slaughter of Midian at the rock of Oreb; and as his rod was upon the sea so shall he lift it up after the manner of Egypt.
27 And it shall come to pass in that day that his burden shall be taken away from off thy shoulder, and his yoke from off thy neck, and the yoke shall be destroyed because of the anointing.
28 He is come to Aiath, he is passed to Migron; at Michmash he hath laid up his carriages.
29 They are gone over the passage; they have taken up their lodging at Geba; Ramath is afraid; Gibeah of Saul is fled.
30 Lift up the voice, O daughter of Gallim; cause it to be heard unto Laish, O poor Anathoth.
31 Madmenah is removed; the inhabitants of Gebim gather themselves to flee.
32 As yet shall he remain at Nob that day; he shall shake his hand against the mount of the daughter of Zion, the hill of Jerusalem.
33 Behold, the Lord, the Lord of Hosts shall lop the bough with terror; and the high ones of stature shall be hewn down; and the haughty shall be humbled.
34 And he shall cut down the thickets of the forests with iron, and Lebanon shall fall by a mighty one.

Date _____
☐ Completed

2 Nephi

Chapter 21

Sight (Memorization) Words

over

Word Pattern

Pattern	-ush
Pattern words in scriptures	**Cush**
Location in chapter	Verse 11
Exceptions to the rule	bush, push
Other words made from this patterns not found in chapter	lush, mush, rush, blush, flush, crush

Phonics Application

- *Short vowel sounds:* the sound of the letter phonetically (versus the long sound or name of the letter).
  - The short sound of U (example: c**u**p)
- *Consonant-Vowel-Blend and Blend-Vowel-Blend:* these patterns are the merging together of sounds to make words. A blend is the combination of two (or more) consonants together. These are the blends: BL, CL, FL, GL, PL, SL, BR, CR, DR, FR, GR, PR, TR, SC, SK, SM, SN, SP, ST, SW, TW.
- *Consonant Diagraphs:* diagraphs are two letters that make one sound. The diagraphs are TH, CH, SH, WH.
- *Complex Consonants:* blends that include three consonants, two consonants that sounds like a single letter, and consonant and vowel clusters. The complex consonants are QU, TCH, CK.

Recommended (Age Appropriate) Reading Chunks

- Verses 1–8
- Verses 9–16

Gospel Principle Review/Activity

- What is an "ensign" and what ensign will the Lord raise to gather Israel?
- *Activity:* The Lord uses the example of a tree often when trying to describe the gospel. Label the parts of a tree (leaves, branches, trunk, roots). Next to those labels, write what you think each part represents.

Word Patterns

ush

Lesson 43: words made with –ush word pattern.
Use alphabet letters to create words.

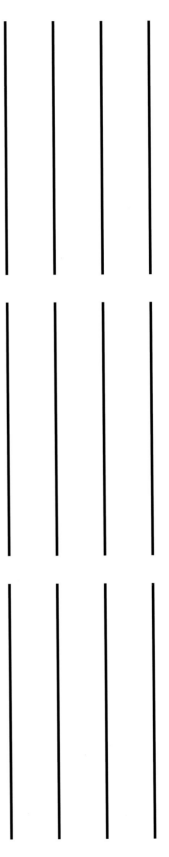

2 Nephi 21

1 And there shall come forth a rod out of the stem of Jesse, and a branch shall grow out of his roots.

2 And the Spirit of the Lord shall rest upon him, the spirit of wisdom and understanding, the spirit of counsel and might, the spirit of knowledge and of the fear of the Lord;

3 And shall make him of quick understanding in the fear of the Lord; and he shall not judge after the sight of his eyes, neither reprove after the hearing of his ears.

4 But with righteousness shall he judge the poor, and reprove with equity for the meek of the earth; and he shall smite the earth with the rod of his mouth, and with the breath of his lips shall he slay the wicked.

5 And righteousness shall be the girdle of his loins, and faithfulness the girdle of his reins.

6 The wolf also shall dwell with the lamb, and the leopard shall lie down with the kid, and the calf and the young lion and fatling together; and a little child shall lead them.

7 And the cow and the bear shall feed; their young ones shall lie down together; and the lion shall eat straw like the ox.

8 And the sucking child shall play on the hole of the asp, and the weaned child shall put his hand on the cockatrice's den.

Date _____

☐ Completed

9 They shall not hurt nor destroy in all my holy mountain, for the earth shall be full of the knowledge of the Lord, as the waters cover the sea.

10 And in that day there shall be a root of Jesse, which shall stand for an ensign of the people; to it shall the Gentiles seek; and his rest shall be glorious.

11 And it shall come to pass in that day that the Lord shall set his hand again the second time to recover the remnant of his people which shall be left, from Assyria, and from Egypt, and from Pathros, and from Cush, and from Elam, and from Shinar, and from Hamath, and from the islands of the sea.

12 And he shall set up an ensign for the nations, and shall assemble the outcasts of Israel, and gather together the dispersed of Judah from the four corners of the earth.

13 The envy of Ephraim also shall depart, and the adversaries of Judah shall be cut off; Ephraim shall not envy Judah, and Judah shall not vex Ephraim.

14 But they shall fly upon the shoulders of the Philistines towards the west; they shall spoil them of the east together; they shall lay their hand upon Edom and Moab; and the children of Ammon shall obey them.

15 And the Lord shall utterly destroy the tongue of the Egyptian sea;

and with his mighty wind he shall shake his hand over the river, and shall smite it in the seven streams, and make men go over dry shod.

16 And there shall be a highway for the remnant of his people which shall be left, from Assyria, like as it was to Israel in the day that he came up out of the land of Egypt.

2 Nephi

Chapter 22

Sight (Memorization) Words

said

Word Pattern

Pattern	Exception: -ing (I makes the long E sound)
Pattern words in scriptures	**sing**
Location in chapter	Verse 13
Other words made from this patterns not found in chapter	bing, ding, king, ping, ring, wing, zing, cling, fling, sling, bring, sting, swing, thing

Phonics Application

- *Short vowel sounds:* the sound of the letter phonetically (versus the long sound or name of the letter). The short sound of I (example: h**i**t)
- *Consonant-Vowel-Blend and Blend-Vowel-Blend:* these patterns are the merging together of sounds to make words. A blend is the combination of two (or more) consonants together. These are the blends: BL, CL, FL, GL, PL, SL, BR, CR, DR, FR, GR, PR, TR, SC, SK, SM, SN, SP, ST, SW, TW.
- *Consonant Diagraphs:* diagraphs are two letters that make one sound. The diagraphs are TH, CH, SH, WH.
- *Complex Consonants:* blends that include three consonants, two consonants that sounds like a single letter, and consonant and vowel clusters. The complex consonants are QU, TCH, CK.

Recommended (Age Appropriate) Reading Chunks

- Verses 1–6

Gospel Principle Review/Activity

- *Activity:* What "excellent things" has the Lord done for you and your family? With the help of a parent, record these blessings in your journal and perhaps offer a pray of thanksgiving to the Lord.

Word Patterns

_ing

Lesson 44: words made with –ing word pattern.
Use alphabet letters to create words.

193

2 Nephi 22

1 And in that day thou shalt say: O Lord, I will praise thee; though thou wast angry with me thine anger is turned away, and thou comfortedest me.

2 Behold, God is my salvation; I will trust, and not be afraid; for the Lord Jehovah is my strength and my song; he also has become my salvation.

3 Therefore, with joy shall ye draw water out of the wells of salvation.

4 And in that day shall ye say: Praise the Lord, call upon his name, declare his doings among the people, make mention that his name is exalted.

5 Sing unto the Lord; for he hath done excellent things; this is known in all the earth.

6 Cry out and shout, thou inhabitant of Zion; for great is the Holy One of Israel in the midst of thee.

Date _____

☐ Completed

2 Nephi

Chapter 23

Sight (Memorization) Words

no

Word Pattern

Pattern	-ith
Pattern words in scriptures	**with**
Location in chapter	Verse 9
Exception to the rule	myth
Other words made from this patterns not found in chapter	Smith

Phonics Application

- *Short vowel sounds:* the sound of the letter phonetically (versus the long sound or name of the letter).
  - The short sound of I (example: h**i**t)
- *Consonant-Vowel-Blend and Blend-Vowel-Blend:* these patterns are the merging together of sounds to make words. A blend is the combination of two (or more) consonants together. These are the blends: BL, CL, FL, GL, PL, SL, BR, CR, DR, FR, GR, PR, TR, SC, SK, SM, SN, SP, ST, SW, TW.
- *Consonant Diagraphs:* diagraphs are two letters that make one sound. The diagraphs are TH, CH, SH, WH.
- *Complex Consonants:* blends that include three consonants, two consonants that sounds like a single letter, and consonant and vowel clusters. The complex consonants are QU, TCH, CK.

Recommended (Age Appropriate) Reading Chunks

- Verses 1–10
- Verses 11–17
- Verses 18–22

Gospel Principle Review/Activity

- Isaiah talks a lot about Babylon. What was wrong with Babylon?
- *Activity:* The Lord speaks of the stars and the constellations.
  - What are constellations? Learn what a constellation is and study the eighty-eight types of constellations.
  - During nighttime, lie out and see if you can see them.
  - See if you can create your own constellation.

Word Patterns

_ith

Lesson 45: words made with –ith word pattern.
Use alphabet letters to create words.

2 Nephi 23

1 The burden of Babylon, which Isaiah the son of Amoz did see.

2 Lift ye up a banner upon the high mountain, exalt the voice unto them, shake the hand, that they may go into the gates of the nobles.

3 I have commanded my sanctified ones, I have also called my mighty ones, for mine anger is not upon them that rejoice in my highness.

4 The noise of the multitude in the mountains like as of a great people, a tumultuous noise of the kingdoms of nations gathered together, the Lord of Hosts mustereth the hosts of the battle.

5 They come from a far country, from the end of heaven, yea, the Lord, and the weapons of his indignation, to destroy the whole land.

6 Howl ye, for the day of the Lord is at hand; it shall come as a destruction from the Almighty.

7 Therefore shall all hands be faint, every man's heart shall melt;

8 And they shall be afraid; pangs and sorrows shall take hold of them; they shall be amazed one at another; their faces shall be as flames.

9 Behold, the day of the Lord cometh, cruel both with wrath and fierce anger, to lay the land desolate; and he shall destroy the sinners thereof out of it.

10 For the stars of heaven and the constellations thereof shall not give their light; the sun shall be darkened in his going forth, and the moon shall not cause her light to shine.

Date _____
☐ Completed

11 And I will punish the world for evil, and the wicked for their iniquity; I will cause the arrogancy of the proud to cease, and will lay down the haughtiness of the terrible.

12 I will make a man more precious than fine gold; even a man than the golden wedge of Ophir.

13 Therefore, I will shake the heavens, and the earth shall remove out of her place, in the wrath of the Lord of Hosts, and in the day of his fierce anger.

14 And it shall be as the chased roe, and as a sheep that no man taketh up; and they shall every man turn to his own people, and flee every one into his own land.

15 Every one that is proud shall be thrust through; yea, and every one that is joined to the wicked shall fall by the sword.

16 Their children also shall be dashed to pieces before their eyes; their houses shall be spoiled and their wives ravished.

17 Behold, I will stir up the Medes against them, which shall not regard silver and gold, nor shall they delight in it.

Date _____
☐ Completed

18 Their bows shall also dash the young men to pieces; and they shall have no pity on the fruit of the womb; their eyes shall not spare children.

19 And Babylon, the glory of kingdoms, the beauty of the Chaldees' excellency, shall be as when God overthrew Sodom and Gomorrah.

20 It shall never be inhabited, neither shall it be dwelt in from generation to generation: neither shall the Arabian pitch tent there; neither shall the shepherds make their fold there.

21 But wild beasts of the desert shall lie there; and their houses shall be full of doleful creatures; and owls shall dwell there, and satyrs shall dance there.

22 And the wild beasts of the islands shall cry in their desolate houses, and dragons in their pleasant palaces; and her time is near to come, and her day shall not be prolonged. For I will destroy her speedily; yea, for I will be merciful unto my people, but the wicked shall perish.

Date _____

☐ Completed

2 Nephi

Chapter 24

Sight (Memorization) Words

so

Word Pattern

Pattern	-est
Pattern words in scriptures	**rest**
Location in chapter	Verse 7
Exceptions to the rule	guest, quest, dressed
Other words made from this patterns not found in chapter	best, lest, nest, pest, test, vest, west, zest, blest, crest, chest

Phonics Application

- *Words that end with vowels:* when a word ends with a vowel and it is the only vowel in the word, the vowel is usually a LONG vowel, or a vowel that says its name (example: s**o**).
- *Short vowel sounds:* the sound of the letter phonetically (versus the long sound or name of the letter).
  - The short sound of E (example: b**e**d)
- *Consonant-Vowel-Blend and Blend-Vowel-Blend:* these patterns are the merging together of sounds to make words. A blend is the combination of two (or more) consonants together. These are the blends: BL, CL, FL, GL, PL, SL, BR, CR, DR, FR, GR, PR, TR, SC, SK, SM, SN, SP, ST, SW, TW.
- *Consonant Diagraphs:* diagraphs are two letters that make one sound. The diagraphs are TH, CH, SH, WH.
- *Complex Consonants:* blends that include three consonants, two consonants that sounds like a single letter, and consonant and vowel clusters. The complex consonants are QU, TCH, CK.

Recommended (Age Appropriate) Reading Chunks

- Verses 1–7
- Verses 8–15
- Verses 16–23
- Verses 24–32

Gospel Principle Review/Activity

- What will happen to Lucifer (Satan) during the Millennium?
- Why is Lucifer a "Son of the Morning"? What was he like before he was cast out of heaven?
- *Activity:* Write in your journal what you think life would be like is there were no evil and Satan were bound.

Word Patterns

_____ est

Lesson 46: words made with –est word pattern.
Use alphabet letters to create words.

2 Nephi 24

1 For the Lord will have mercy on Jacob, and will yet choose Israel, and set them in their own land; and the strangers shall be joined with them, and they shall cleave to the house of Jacob.

2 And the people shall take them and bring them to their place; yea, from far unto the ends of the earth; and they shall return to their lands of promise. And the house of Israel shall possess them, and the land of the Lord shall be for servants and handmaids; and they shall take them captives unto whom they were captives; and they shall rule over their oppressors.

3 And it shall come to pass in that day that the Lord shall give thee rest, from thy sorrow, and from thy fear, and from the hard bondage wherein thou wast made to serve.

4 And it shall come to pass in that day, that thou shalt take up this proverb against the king of Babylon, and say: How hath the oppressor ceased, the golden city ceased!

5 The Lord hath broken the staff of the wicked, the scepters of the rulers.

6 He who smote the people in wrath with a continual stroke, he that ruled the nations in anger, is persecuted, and none hindereth.

7 The whole earth is at rest, and is quiet; they break forth into singing.

Date _____

☐ Completed

8 Yea, the fir–trees rejoice at thee, and also the cedars of Lebanon, saying: Since thou art laid down no feller is come up against us.

9 Hell from beneath is moved for thee to meet thee at thy coming; it stirreth up the dead for thee, even all the chief ones of the earth; it hath raised up from their thrones all the kings of the nations.

10 All they shall speak and say unto thee: Art thou also become weak as we? Art thou become like unto us?

11 Thy pomp is brought down to the grave; the noise of thy viols is not heard; the worm is spread under thee, and the worms cover thee.

12 How art thou fallen from heaven, O Lucifer, son of the morning! Art thou cut down to the ground, which did weaken the nations!

13 For thou hast said in thy heart: I will ascend into heaven, I will exalt my throne above the stars of God; I will sit also upon the mount of the congregation, in the sides of the north;

14 I will ascend above the heights of the clouds; I will be like the Most High.

15 Yet thou shalt be brought down to hell, to the sides of the pit.

Date _____

☐ Completed

16 They that see thee shall narrowly look upon thee, and shall consider thee, and shall say: Is this the man that made the earth to tremble, that

did shake kingdoms?

17 And made the world as a wilderness, and destroyed the cities thereof, and opened not the house of his prisoners?

18 All the kings of the nations, yea, all of them, lie in glory, every one of them in his own house.

19 But thou art cast out of thy grave like an abominable branch, and the remnant of those that are slain, thrust through with a sword, that go down to the stones of the pit; as a carcass trodden under feet.

20 Thou shalt not be joined with them in burial, because thou hast destroyed thy land and slain thy people; the seed of evil–doers shall never be renowned.

21 Prepare slaughter for his children for the iniquities of their fathers, that they do not rise, nor possess the land, nor fill the face of the world with cities.

22 For I will rise up against them, saith the Lord of Hosts, and cut off from Babylon the name, and remnant, and son, and nephew, saith the Lord.

23 I will also make it a possession for the bittern, and pools of water; and I will sweep it with the besom of destruction, saith the Lord of Hosts.

---

24 The Lord of Hosts hath sworn, saying: Surely as I have thought, so shall it come to pass; and as I have purposed, so shall it stand—

25 That I will bring the Assyrian in my land, and upon my mountains tread him under foot; then shall his yoke depart from off them, and his burden depart from off their shoulders.

26 This is the purpose that is purposed upon the whole earth; and this is the hand that is stretched out upon all nations.

27 For the Lord of Hosts hath purposed, and who shall disannul? And his hand is stretched out, and who shall turn it back?

28 In the year that king Ahaz died was this burden.

29 Rejoice not thou, whole Palestina, because the rod of him that smote thee is broken; for out of the serpent's root shall come forth a cockatrice, and his fruit shall be a fiery flying serpent.

30 And the first–born of the poor shall feed, and the needy shall lie down in safety; and I will kill thy root with famine, and he shall slay thy remnant.

31 Howl, O gate; cry, O city; thou, whole Palestina, art dissolved; for there shall come from the north a smoke, and none shall be alone in his appointed times.

32 What shall then answer the messengers of the nations? That the Lord hath founded Zion, and the poor of his people shall trust in it.

Date _____

☐ Completed

Date _____

☐ Completed

2 Nephi

Chapter 25

Sight (Memorization) Words

Word Pattern

Pattern	-ust
Pattern words in scriptures	**must**
Location in chapter	Verses 16, 29–30
Other words made from this patterns not found in chapter	dust, just, lust, rust

Phonics Application

- *Rules:* for words that end in OLD, the O makes the long O sound.
- *Short vowel sounds:* the sound of the letter phonetically (versus the long sound or name of the letter).
  - The short sound of U (example: c**u**p)
- *Consonant-Vowel-Blend and Blend-Vowel-Blend:* these patterns are the merging together of sounds to make words. A blend is the combination of two (or more) consonants together. These are the blends: BL, CL, FL, GL, PL, SL, BR, CR, DR, FR, GR, PR, TR, SC, SK, SM, SN, SP, ST, SW, TW.
- *Consonant Diagraphs:* diagraphs are two letters that make one sound. The diagraphs are TH, CH, SH, WH.
- *Complex Consonants:* blends that include three consonants, two consonants that sounds like a single letter, and consonant and vowel clusters. The complex consonants are QU, TCH, CK.

Recommended (Age Appropriate) Reading Chunks

- Verses 1–4
- Verses 5–8
- Verses 9–13
- Verses 14–17
- Verses 18–20
- Verses 21–26
- Verses 27–30

Gospel Principle Review/Activity

- Why does Nephi like to study Isaiah so much?
- What do we have to do in order to be saved by grace?
- Why does Nephi talk, rejoice, preach and prophesy of Christ?
- *Activity:* Nephi likes to study the words of Isaiah.
  - Who is your favorite prophet to study? Why?
  - Share your favorite scripture from your favorite prophet in your next Family Home Evening.

Word Patterns

ust

Lesson 47: words made with –ust word pattern.
Use alphabet letters to create words.

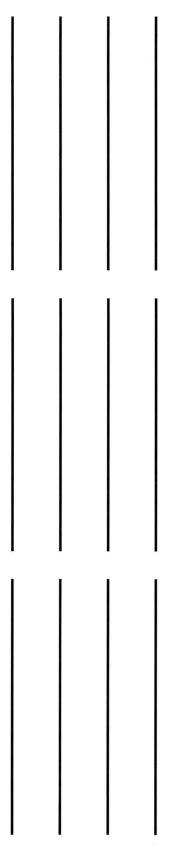

2 Nephi 25

1 Now I, Nephi, do speak somewhat concerning the words which I have written, which have been spoken by the mouth of Isaiah. For behold, Isaiah spake many things which were hard for many of my people to understand; for they know not concerning the manner of prophesying among the Jews.

2 For I, Nephi, have not taught them many things concerning the manner of the Jews; for their works were works of darkness, and their doings were doings of abominations.

3 Wherefore, I write unto my people, unto all those that shall receive hereafter these things which I write, that they may know the judgments of God, that they come upon all nations, according to the word which he hath spoken.

4 Wherefore, hearken, O my people, which are of the house of Israel, and give ear unto my words; for because the words of Isaiah are not plain unto you, nevertheless they are plain unto all those that are filled with the spirit of prophecy. But I give unto you a prophecy, according to the spirit which is in me; wherefore I shall prophesy according to the plainness which hath been with me from the time that I came out from Jerusalem with my father; for behold, my soul delighteth in plainness unto my people, that they may learn.

5 Yea, and my soul delighteth in the words of Isaiah, for I came out from Jerusalem, and mine eyes hath beheld the things of the Jews, and I know that the Jews do understand the things of the prophets, and there is none other people that understand the things which were spoken unto the Jews like unto them, save it be that they are taught after the manner of the things of the Jews.

6 But behold, I, Nephi, have not taught my children after the manner of the Jews; but behold, I, of myself, have dwelt at Jerusalem, wherefore I know concerning the regions round about; and I have made mention unto my children concerning the judgments of God, which hath come to pass among the Jews, unto my children, according to all that which Isaiah hath spoken, and I do not write them.

7 But behold, I proceed with mine own prophecy, according to my plainness; in the which I know that no man can err; nevertheless, in the days that the prophecies of Isaiah shall be fulfilled men shall know of a surety, at the times when they shall come to pass.

8 Wherefore, they are of worth unto the children of men, and he that supposeth that they are not, unto them will I speak particularly, and confine the words unto mine own people; for I know that they shall be of great worth unto them in the last days; for in that day shall they understand them; wherefore, for their good have I written them.

Date _____
☐ Completed

Date _____
☐ Completed

9 And as one generation hath been destroyed among the Jews because of iniquity, even so have they been destroyed from generation to generation according to their iniquities; and never hath any of them been destroyed save it were foretold them by the prophets of the Lord.

10 Wherefore, it hath been told them concerning the destruction which should come upon them, immediately after my father left Jerusalem; nevertheless, they hardened their hearts; and according to my prophecy they have been destroyed, save it be those which are carried away captive into Babylon.

11 And now this I speak because of the spirit which is in me. And notwithstanding they have been carried away they shall return again, and possess the land of Jerusalem; wherefore, they shall be restored again to the land of their inheritance.

12 But, behold, they shall have wars, and rumors of wars; and when the day cometh that the Only Begotten of the Father, yea, even the Father of heaven and of earth, shall manifest himself unto them in the flesh, behold, they will reject him, because of their iniquities, and the hardness of their hearts, and the stiffness of their necks.

13 Behold, they will crucify him; and after he is laid in a sepulchre for the space of three days he shall rise from the dead, with healing in his wings; and all those who shall believe on his name shall be saved in the kingdom of God. Wherefore, my soul delighteth to prophesy concerning him, for I have seen his day, and my heart doth magnify his holy name.

---

14 And behold it shall come to pass that after the Messiah hath risen from the dead, and hath manifested himself unto his people, unto as many as will believe on his name, behold, Jerusalem shall be destroyed again; for wo unto them that fight against God and the people of his church.

15 Wherefore, the Jews shall be scattered among all nations; yea, and also Babylon shall be destroyed; wherefore, the Jews shall be scattered by other nations.

16 And after they have been scattered, and the Lord God hath scourged them by other nations for the space of many generations, yea, even down from generation to generation until they shall be persuaded to believe in Christ, the Son of God, and the atonement, which is infinite for all mankind—and when that day shall come that they shall believe in Christ, and worship the Father in his name, with pure hearts and clean hands, and look not forward any more for another Messiah, then, at that time, the day will come that it must needs be expedient that they should believe these things.

17 And the Lord will set his hand again the second time to restore his people from their lost and fallen state. Wherefore, he will proceed to do a marvelous work and a wonder among the children of men.

Date _____
☐ Completed

Date _____
☐ Completed

18 Wherefore, he shall bring forth his words unto them, which words shall judge them at the last day, for they shall be given them for the purpose of convincing them of the true Messiah, who was rejected by them; and unto the convincing of them that they need not look forward any more for a Messiah to come, for there should not any come, save it should be a false Messiah which should deceive the people; for there is save one Messiah spoken of by the prophets, and that Messiah is he who should be rejected of the Jews.

19 For according to the words of the prophets, the Messiah cometh in six hundred years from the time that my father left Jerusalem; and according to the words of the prophets, and also the word of the angel of God, his name shall be Jesus Christ, the Son of God.

20 And now, my brethren, I have spoken plainly that ye cannot err. And as the Lord God liveth that brought Israel up out of the land of Egypt, and gave unto Moses power that he should heal the nations after they had been bitten by the poisonous serpents, if they would cast their eyes unto the serpent which he did raise up before them, and also gave him power that he should smite the rock and the water should come forth; yea, behold I say unto you, that as these things are true, and as the Lord God liveth, there is none other name given under heaven save it be this Jesus Christ, of which I have spoken, whereby man can be saved.

21 Wherefore, for this cause hath the Lord God promised unto me that these things which I write shall be kept and preserved, and handed down unto my seed, from generation to generation, that the promise may be fulfilled unto Joseph, that his seed should never perish as long as the earth should stand.

22 Wherefore, these things shall go from generation to generation as long as the earth shall stand; and they shall go according to the will and pleasure of God; and the nations who shall possess them shall be judged of them according to the words which are written.

23 For we labor diligently to write, to persuade our children, and also our brethren, to believe in Christ, and to be reconciled to God; for we know that it is by grace that we are saved, after all we can do.

24 And, notwithstanding we believe in Christ, we keep the law of Moses, and look forward with steadfastness unto Christ, until the law shall be fulfilled.

25 For, for this end was the law given; wherefore the law hath become dead unto us, and we are made alive in Christ because of our faith; yet we keep the law because of the commandments.

26 And we talk of Christ, we rejoice in Christ, we preach of Christ, we prophesy of Christ, and we write according to our prophecies, that our children may know to what source they may look for a remission of their sins.

Date _____
☐ Completed

Date _____
☐ Completed

27 Wherefore, we speak concerning the law that our children may know the deadness of the law; and they, by knowing the deadness of the law, may look forward unto that life which is in Christ, and know for what end the law was given. And after the law is fulfilled in Christ, that they need not harden their hearts against him when the law ought to be done away.

28 And now behold, my people, ye are a stiffnecked people; wherefore, I have spoken plainly unto you, that ye cannot misunderstand. And the words which I have spoken shall stand as a testimony against you; for they are sufficient to teach any man the right way; for the right way is to believe in Christ and deny him not; for by denying him ye also deny the prophets and the law.

29 And now behold, I say unto you that the right way is to believe in Christ, and deny him not; and Christ is the Holy One of Israel; wherefore ye must bow down before him, and worship him with all your might, mind, and strength, and your whole soul; and if ye do this ye shall in nowise be cast out.

30 And, inasmuch as it shall be expedient, ye must keep the performances and ordinances of God until the law shall be fulfilled which was given unto Moses.

Date _____

☐ Completed

2 Nephi

Chapter 26—Review

Sight (Memorization) Words

son	walk	thee	out	over	said	no	so	what

Word Pattern

ALL SHORT VOWEL WORDS (without any other rule)

> A Patterns: -ack, -aft, -all, -amp, -and, -ang, -ank, -ant, -art, -ash, -ask, -ass, -ast, -ath
> E Patterns: -eck, -eft, -elf, -ell, -elt, -end, -ent, -elp, -ept, -esh, -ess, -est
> I Patterns: -ich, -ick, -iff, -ift, -ilk, -ill, -ilt, -ing, -ink, -ish, -isk, ist, -itch, -ith
> O Patterns: -ock, -oll, -ond, -ong, -oss, -ost
> U Patterns: -uch, -uck, -uff, -ulf, -ump, -ung, -unk, -unt,, -ush, -ust, -utch

(Note: from this chapter on, every word that has all short sounds without any other rule will be highlighted in blue.)

Phonics Application

- *Short vowel sounds:* the sound of the letter phonetically (versus the long sound or name of the letter).
  - The short sound of A (example: **a**pple)
  - The short sound of E (example: b**e**d)
  - The short sound of I (example: h**i**t)
  - The short sound of O (example: h**o**p)
  - The short sound of U (example: c**u**p)
- *Consonant-Vowel-Blend and Blend-Vowel-Blend:* these patterns are the merging together of sounds to make words. A blend is the combination of two (or more) consonants together. These are the blends: BL, CL, FL, GL, PL, SL, BR, CR, DR, FR, GR, PR, TR, SC, SK, SM, SN, SP, ST, SW, TW.
- *Consonant Diagraphs:* diagraphs are two letters that make one sound. The diagraphs are TH, CH, SH, WH.
- *Complex Consonants:* blends that include three consonants, two consonants that sounds like a single letter, and consonant and vowel clusters. The complex consonants are QU, TCH, CK.
- *Doublet:* a special type of across-syllable pattern in which the two consonants are the same.
  - LL (example: ba**ll**)

Recommended (Age Appropriate) Reading Chunks

- Verses 1–5
- Verses 6–9
- Verses 10–14
- Verses 15–18
- Verses 19–24
- Verses 25–30
- Verses 31–33

Gospel Principle Review/Activity

- What does Nephi foresee will happen to his people?
- *Activity:* Nephi makes some prophecies in this chapter about the coming of Christ. Write down when these events occur on the timeline:

Christ's Birth

Word Patterns—Review

Lesson 48 Review: Find the words in the word box in the word search.

J	U	P	P	F	R	W	P	N	E
U	U	A	K	C	E	N	L	I	L
D	R	N	H	R	Y	C	E	B	E
T	N	S	I	N	G	W	H	E	A
D	U	E	M	B	X	Z	I	S	S
R	U	S	F	V	K	K	T	O	
N	S	N	Y	O	T	F	B	F	H
T	E	U	R	J	X	N	H	M	Z
H	C	R	P	Z	S	B	D	R	X
B	S	J	J	W	W	T	K	Y	

Word Box

part

neck

send

help

rush

sing

with

best

must

2 Nephi 26

1 And after Christ shall have risen from the dead he shall show himself unto you, my children, and my beloved brethren; and the words which he shall speak unto you shall be the law which ye shall do.

2 For behold, I say unto you that I have beheld that many generations shall pass away, and there shall be great wars and contentions among my people.

3 And after the Messiah shall come there shall be signs given unto my people of his birth, and also of his death and resurrection; and great and terrible shall that day be unto the wicked, for they shall perish; and they perish because they cast out the prophets, and the saints, and stone them, and slay them; wherefore the cry of the blood of the saints shall ascend up to God from the ground against them.

4 Wherefore, all those who are proud, and that do wickedly, the day that cometh shall burn them up, saith the Lord of Hosts, for they shall be as stubble.

5 And they that kill the prophets, and the saints, the depths of the earth shall swallow them up, saith the Lord of Hosts; and mountains shall cover them, and whirlwinds shall carry them away, and buildings shall fall upon them and crush them to pieces and grind them to powder.

Date _____
☐ Completed

6 And they shall be visited with thunderings, and lightnings, and earthquakes, and all manner of destructions, for the fire of the anger of the Lord shall be kindled against them, and they shall be as stubble, and the day that cometh shall consume them, saith the Lord of Hosts.

7 O the pain, and the anguish of my soul for the loss of the slain of my people! For I, Nephi, have seen it, and it well nigh consumeth me before the presence of the Lord; but I must cry unto my God: Thy ways are just.

8 But behold, the righteous that hearken unto the words of the prophets, and destroy them not, but look forward unto Christ with steadfastness for the signs which are given, notwithstanding all persecution—behold, they are they which shall not perish.

9 But the Son of righteousness shall appear unto them; and he shall heal them, and they shall have peace with him, until three generations shall have passed away, and many of the fourth generation shall have passed away in righteousness.

Date _____
☐ Completed

10 And when these things have passed away a speedy destruction cometh unto my people; for, notwithstanding the pains of my soul, I have seen it; wherefore, I know that it shall come to pass; and they sell themselves for naught; for, for the reward of their pride and their foolishness they shall reap destruction; for because they yield unto the devil and choose works of darkness rather than light, therefore they must go down to hell.

11 For the Spirit of the Lord will not always strive with man. And when

the Spirit ceaseth to strive with man then cometh speedy destruction, and this grieveth my soul.

12 And as I spake concerning the convincing of the Jews, that Jesus is the very Christ, it must needs be that the Gentiles be convinced also that Jesus is the Christ, the Eternal God;

13 And that he manifesteth himself unto all those who believe in him, by the power of the Holy Ghost; yea, unto every nation, kindred, tongue, and people, working mighty miracles, signs, and wonders, among the children of men according to their faith.

14 But behold, I prophesy unto you concerning the last days; concerning the days when the Lord God shall bring these things forth unto the children of men.

___

15 After my seed and the seed of my brethren shall have dwindled in unbelief, and shall have been smitten by the Gentiles; yea, after the Lord God shall have camped against them round about, and shall have laid siege against them with a mount, and raised forts against them; and after they shall have been brought down low in the dust, even that they are not, yet the words of the righteous shall be written, and the prayers of the faithful shall be heard, and all those who have dwindled in unbelief shall not be forgotten.

16 For those who shall be destroyed shall speak unto them out of the ground, and their speech shall be low out of the dust, and their voice shall be as one that hath a familiar spirit; for the Lord God will give unto him power, that he may whisper concerning them, even as it were out of the ground; and their speech shall whisper out of the dust.

17 For thus saith the Lord God: They shall write the things which shall be done among them, and they shall be written and sealed up in a book, and those who have dwindled in unbelief shall not have them, for they seek to destroy the things of God.

18 Wherefore, as those who have been destroyed have been destroyed speedily; and the multitude of their terrible ones shall be as chaff that passeth away—yea, thus saith the Lord God: It shall be at an instant, suddenly—

___

19 And it shall come to pass, that those who have dwindled in unbelief shall be smitten by the hand of the Gentiles.

20 And the Gentiles are lifted up in the pride of their eyes, and have stumbled, because of the greatness of their stumbling block, that they have built up many churches; nevertheless, they put down the power and miracles of God, and preach up unto themselves their own wisdom and their own learning, that they may get gain and grind upon the face of the poor.

21 And there are many churches built up which cause envyings, and strifes, and malice.

22 And there are also secret combinations, even as in times of old, according to the combinations of the devil, for he is the founder of all these

Date _____
☐ Completed

Date _____
☐ Completed

things; yea, the founder of murder, and works of darkness; yea, and he leadeth them by the neck with a flaxen cord, until he bindeth them with his strong cords forever.

23 For behold, my beloved brethren, I say unto you that the Lord God worketh not in darkness.

24 He doeth not anything save it be for the benefit of the world; for he loveth the world, even that he layeth down his own life that he may draw all men unto him. Wherefore, he commandeth none that they shall not partake of his salvation.

25 Behold, doth he cry unto any, saying: Depart from me? Behold, I say unto you, Nay; but he saith: Come unto me all ye ends of the earth, buy milk and honey, without money and without price.

26 Behold, hath he commanded any that they should depart out of the synagogues, or out of the houses of worship? Behold, I say unto you, Nay.

27 Hath he commanded any that they should not partake of his salvation? Behold I say unto you, Nay; but he hath given it free for all men; and he hath commanded his people that they should persuade all men to repentance.

28 Behold, hath the Lord commanded any that they should not partake of his goodness? Behold I say unto you, Nay; but all men are privileged the one like unto the other, and none are forbidden.

29 He commandeth that there shall be no priestcrafts; for, behold, priestcrafts are that men preach and set themselves up for a light unto the world, that they may get gain and praise of the world; but they seek not the welfare of Zion.

30 Behold, the Lord hath forbidden this thing; wherefore, the Lord God hath given a commandment that all men should have charity, which charity is love. And except they should have charity they were nothing. Wherefore, if they should have charity they would not suffer the laborer in Zion to perish.

31 But the laborer in Zion shall labor for Zion; for if they labor for money they shall perish.

32 And again, the Lord God hath commanded that men should not murder; that they should not lie; that they should not steal; that they should not take the name of the Lord their God in vain; that they should not envy; that they should not have malice; that they should not contend one with another; that they should not commit whoredoms; and that they should do none of these things; for whoso doeth them shall perish.

33 For none of these iniquities come of the Lord; for he doeth that which is good among the children of men; and he doeth nothing save it be plain unto the children of men; and he inviteth them all to come unto him and partake of his goodness; and he denieth none that come unto him, black and white, bond and free, male and female; and he remembereth the heathen; and all are alike unto God, both Jew and Gentile.

Date _____
☐ Completed

Date _____
☐ Completed

Date _____
☐ Completed

Endnotes

1. "Every Child Reading: Outreach Kit, Dyslexia: Characteristics and Effective Intervention." Baltimore, MD The International Dyslexia Association, 2005.
2. *LD Online.* Online. Accessed 2006; available from ldonline.org/.
3. Gordon B. Hinckley, "Forgiveness," *Ensign*, Nov. 2005, 81.

Sources Consulted

American Heritage Dictionary—Third Edition. New York, New York: Dell Publishing, 1994.

AVKO Educational Research Foundation. Online. "The Learning Disabilities/Dyslexia Specialists." Accessed February 15, 2005; available from www.speccling.org/Freebies/ie_rule.htm.

Bear, Donald R., Marcia Invernizzi, Shane Templeton, and Francine Johnston. *Words Their Way—Word Study for Phonics, Vocabulary, and Spelling Instruction, 2nd ed.* Columbus, Ohio: Merrill an imprint of Prentice Hall, 2000.

Beck, Isabel, L., Margaret G. McKeown, and Linda Kucan. *Bringing Words to Life, Robust Vocabulary Instruction.* New York, London: The Guilford Press, 2002.

Holy Bible, King James Version. Bible Dictionary. Salt Lake City: The Church of Jesus Christ of Latter-day Saints, 1981.

Book of Mormon. Index. Salt Lake City: The Church of Jesus Christ of Latter-day Saints,1981.

Cook, Vivian. Online. "I Before E Rule." *Writing Systems.* Accessed May 25, 2006; available from homepage. ntlworld.com/vivian.c/EnglishSpellingSystem/IbeforeE.htm.

Cunningham, Bob. Online. "Exceptions to the Rule 'I before E Except After C.'" Accessed February 23, 2002; available from alt-usage-english.org/I_before_E.html.

Doyle, Dennis. Online. "Phonics, Syllable and Accent Rules." Accessed May 25, 2006; available from english. glendale.cc.ca.us/phonics.rules.html.

Egan, Sherry. Reading Specialist, the Waterford School. Personal Interview. May 2006.

Ganske, Kathy. *Word Journeys—Assessment-Guided Phonics, Spelling, and Vocabulary Instruction.* New York, London: Gilford Press, 2000.

"A Gold Mine of Phonics and phonemic Awareness Worksheets." *Tampa Read.* Online. Accessed May 25, 2006; available from www.tampareads.com/phonics/phonicsindex.htm.

Hayes, Georgia. Online. *Christian Center School.* Accessed May 1, 2006; available from cceschool.org/hayes/ Phonics%20Charts.htm.

"I Before E Except After C." *Wikipedia.* Accessed May 23, 2006; available from en.wikipedia.org/wiki/I_before_e_except_after_c.

LD Online. Accessed 2006; available from ldonline.org/.